DELIA SMITH'S BOOK OF CAKES

Delia Smith is one of the most popular cookery experts writing today.

Justly famous for her phenomenally successful BBC TV series, *Delia Smith's Cookery Course*, for her regular column in the *Evening News* (and before that in the *Evening Standard*), she has a huge and devoted following.

On top of her television and newspaper journalism, she has delighted millions of cooks the world over with her many publications, including the classic paperbacks, FRUGAL FOOD, HOW TO CHEAT AT COOKING and THE EVENING STANDARD COOKBOOK—all available from Coronet.

Front cover shows Cheesecake with Fresh Strawberries, Meringues, Easter Simnel Cake, All-in-one Sponge, Fruit Bran Loaf, Devonshire Scones, Ginger Oat Biscuits, Viennese Tartlets.

Back cover shows Wedding Cake, Traditional Dundee Cake and Chocolate Log with Chestnut Filling.

Delia Smith's Book of Cakes

CORONET BOOKS
Hodder and Stoughton

Copyright © 1977 by Delia Smith

First published 1977 by Hodder and
Stoughton Limited

Coronet edition 1978
Second impression 1980

Printed and bound in Great Britain for
Hodder and Stoughton Paperbacks, a
division of Hodder and Stoughton Ltd.,
Mill Road, Dunton Green, Sevenoaks,
Kent (Editorial Office: 47 Bedford
Square, London, WC1 3DP) by
Richard Clay (The Chaucer Press) Ltd,
Bungay, Suffolk

ISBN 0 340 22158 5

Grateful thanks to Caroline Liddell
for all the help with the testing,
and to Gwyneth Phillips
for typing the manuscript and
helping with the proof.

Illustrations by Robin Lawrie

CONTENTS

LOAF CAKES, TEA BREADS etc

FAMILY CAKES

WHOLEFOOD CAKES

CHOCOLATEY CAKES   89

CAKES FOR OCCASIONS   105

LITTLE CAKES 133

BISCUITS 165

PUDDING CAKES

CHEESECAKE

INDEX

CONVERSION TABLES

WEIGHTS

½ oz	10 g (grams)
1	25
1½	40
2	50
2½	60
3	75
4	110
4½	125
5	150
6	175
7	200
8	225
9	250
10	275
12	350
1 lb	450
1½	700
2	900
3	1 kg 350 g

VOLUME

2 fl oz	55 ml
3 fl oz	75
5 fl oz (¼ pint)	150
½ pint	275
¾ pint	425
1 pint	570
1¾ pints	1 litre
(2 pint basin = 1 litre)	

TEMPERATURES

Mark 1	275 °F	140 °C
2	300	150
3	325	170
4	350	180
5	375	190
6	400	200
7	425	220
8	450	230

MEASUREMENTS

⅛ in	3 mm (millimetre)
¼ in	½ cm (centimetre)
½	1
¾	2
1	2·5
1¼	3
1½	4
1¾	4·5
2	5
3	7·5
4	10
5	13
6	15
7	18
8	20
9	23
10	25·5
11	28
12	30

All these are *approximate* conversions, which have been either rounded up or down. In a few recipes it has been necessary to modify them very slightly.

Introduction

Why a cakes book, you might be thinking. So let me explain first of all that it was *me* who needed a cakes book. Often when I wanted to make a cake I had to hunt through all my other cookery books first, and when I tried to buy an appropriate book on the subject I never seemed to find quite what I wanted. The logical answer seemed to be to set about compiling a special book of cakes of my own.

It's also a subject, or rather an area of cooking, that appears to be shrouded in a mystique of its own. People sometimes assume, quite wrongly, that cake-making is something you either have a gift for or you don't, as the case may be. As far as I'm concerned all that's needed is a simple set of non-contradictory explanations coupled with reliable recipes. Provided the instructions are followed to the letter, *anyone* at all can make a cake.

In this book I've tried to set out the whys and wherefores of cake-making as clearly as possible, for the simple reason I've been so often left wondering myself. If I've read in a book 'how to avoid curdling' my immediate reaction has always been— why should I? Why shouldn't it curdle? And because it frequently doesn't tell me why, I have attempted here not to leave stones like that unturned.

It has not been my intention to offer a world-wide catalogue of cakes: this is simply a selection of my own particular favourites. It never ceases to amaze me how popular cakes are— when I demonstrate a cake on television, we invariably get twice the number of requests for the recipe than for any other kind. Perhaps the gloomier the state of the economy gets, the more we need cheering up with a friendly cake now and then? Speaking of economy, of course, it *is* much cheaper to make cakes at home even taking the cost of the oven into account— and all the more so if we revive the old tradition of batch-baking, and whip up a supply of scones and biscuits at the same time.

Recently I bought two very ordinary supermarket cakes, a ginger cake and a honey cake, to do a comparative costing. I am here to tell you that homemade the Damp Gingerbread (on page 56) and the Honey and Spice Cake (on page 73) worked

14

out at exactly 50 per cent cheaper than their supermarket counterparts.

But perhaps most important of all, I think cakes are often symbols of love and friendship. If someone actually goes to the trouble of baking a cake specially for family or friends, the recipient can't fail to feel spoiled and cared-for. It's true, too, that now all the so-called luxuries of life are receding from our grasp, we are returning to some of the more simple pleasures—like a family kitchen filled with the warm and welcoming aroma of home baking. Now there's a pleasure no shop-bought cake, however expensive, can match!

IMPORTANT INFORMATION

Before making any cake in this book for the first time, please read through the following information—it won't take a minute and it might be very helpful.

1 Ovens

Regrettably ovens vary, so that cooking times given in recipes can only be approximate. In fact I have cooked the same cake in the same oven, and on each occasion the cooking time varied slightly. If, however, you find there's a great deal of difference in your oven from the cooking time given in any recipe, it might be worth having it checked. Also it's most important that ovens with cakes in them should be *left alone*. I know it's hard. You'll feel cut off, want to know what's happening—but my advice is to put a kitchen timer on and go away, because it's that crafty peep that will send cold air rushing in, and the cake might sink. Why spend all that time and trouble and then spoil it in a matter of seconds? So never open the oven door until the cake is at least three-quarters cooked according to the time given. Finally, I have given temperature conversions in this book, but in general if you have a centigrade oven and are not sure about conversions, invest in an oven thermometer and keep it on the centre shelf so that you can see at a glance the temperature in fahrenheit too.

2 *Equipment*

First and foremost *cake tins* are of paramount importance. The reason for so many failed cakes is that the size of tin was incorrect for the mixture. Whenever I hear a tale of woe, it's the first question I ask and often the answer is 'Oh, I didn't have a tin that size.' It's understandable enough—in this country there are so many wretched cake tin sizes, the mind boggles. Why manufacturers cannot agree on a rounding-up of sizes I can't imagine, and I just long for the day when there are fewer variations on the market so that people can follow recipes more accurately. Anyway in this book all cakes (apart from sponge cakes) can be made in tin sizes that are $\frac{1}{2}$-inch different either way from that stated. For the most part I have used 7- or 8-inch round tins throughout, which seems to me to be the most universal. And when we are all utterly and completely metric, the fractional difference between 18 cm and 7 inches (or 20 cm and 8 inches) will not make any difference to these recipes.

Types of cake tin: the more solid the better, and the longer they'll last. The depth is important for sponge tins, because if there isn't enough depth the cakes won't rise (also sponge tins with rotating cutters which are meant to loosen the base of the sponge are a waste of time to my mind—provided you grease and line a tin properly you won't have any problems). If you buy coated non-stick pans, my advice is to ignore the non-stick surface because I've found that traditional methods of greasing and base-lining are still by far the most reliable. Some people have a theory that baking-tins shouldn't be washed. I do always wash mine thoroughly and dry them thoroughly afterwards, because I find they get dirty even stored away in a cupboard—and I'm happy to say they haven't suffered in any way.

3 *Other Equipment*

Large, roomy mixing bowls are needed for cakes requiring lots of air (more about that later). Then wooden spoons for mixing, large metal spoons for folding, and rubber spatula for scraping bowls absolutely clean.

Baking trays: good and solid, for biscuits.

Whisks: the purist will always advocate a wire balloon whisk, and I'd agree that nothing incorporates air into eggs etc as well as one of these. However, it's hard work, and more often than not I'm prepared to sacrifice a little bit of air and conserve my strength by using an electric hand-whisk, which is very quick and efficient.

Wire cooling trays are most important. When you remove cakes from their tins the air needs to circulate all round, and if you stand them on flat surfaces instead the bases can become steamy and soggy.

Measuring jugs: by far the easiest way to measure by volume is to use a glass measuring jug—if you stand it on a flat surface you can see at a glance when you have the correct amount of liquid.

Rolling pin: an old-fashioned wooden rolling pin is best of all, and the longer the better so that you can roll out scone and biscuit mixes smoothly and evenly.

Plain and fluted cutters: for small cakes, biscuits and scones it's very helpful to have a set of pastry cutters, a mixture of plain and fluted. And remember, when you're cutting out, never to twist the cutter—just give it a sharp tap as you cut and lift it straightaway. Twisting will result in some very odd shapes!

Palette knife is something I couldn't live without. Not only does it scrape, spread and smooth, but it's invaluable for lifting cakes and biscuits from the baking tray and for sliding round the edges of cakes to loosen them before you turn them out. I have a rather special one with a serrated edge along one side—

so mine actually cuts cakes (and bread) very efficiently too. It's made by a firm called Victorinox and if you want to know how to get hold of one write to Mr. J. Leslie, Lesway, 49 St. James's Street, Piccadilly, London SW1A 1JT.

Nylon piping bag with one or two plain or starred nozzles is useful if you really want to 'go mad' with the decorations. Also it's essential for éclairs (*see* page 140) to get them exactly the right shape.

Sieves: absolutely essential, but I find the round, wooden-framed kind a bit on the expensive side. So I make do with two or three ordinary nylon ones for flour which I *always* sift.

Proper scales: if you haven't got some scales in your kitchen, this book is of no use to you. It's virtually impossible to make cakes without weighing the ingredients first. Proper balance scales are expensive but they *do* last a lifetime, unlike the flimsy spring scales with needle indicators. These are so often unreliable, and when they need replacing work out more expensive in the long run. It's also possible to buy a set of metric weights now—if you ever get around to going metric!

NOTES ON INGREDIENTS

Flour

There are four different kinds of flour used in this book. *Strong flour* is good for yeast cookery, and puff and flaky pastry. Briefly, and without getting too technical, strong flour has a higher protein content than ordinary flour. When liquid is added a better quantity of gluten is formed, which will produce a larger volume of dough and a light, open texture. Strong flour is *not* essential though, and when it's not available ordinary soft flour can be used.

Plain flour: this is ordinary 'soft' household flour, with a lower protein content than strong flour—so it's more suitable for cakes, pastries and biscuits where a finer, shorter texture is needed.

Self-raising flour is plain soft flour which has a standard amount of raising agent added to it. It's very convenient and has just the right balance of raising agent for quite a number of cakes. Where more or less raising powder is needed plain flour and the correct amount of baking powder are given in the recipe.

Wholewheat flour: since doctors and medical scientists the world over seem to agree that lack of fibre is a major shortcoming of our modern highly-refined diet, wholewheat flour (and wholewheat bread) are becoming more and more desirable and available. The facts are well-known: in wholewheat flour nothing has been added and nothing taken away—it is quite simply flour milled from the whole wheat grain. I find wholefood cookery very challenging, and am delighted with the success of the wholewheat flour recipes (*see* page 77).

Baking Powder

Proprietary brands of baking powder usually contain bicarbonate of soda plus another acid reacting chemical, like cream of tartar. But in some recipes where less raising power is needed, bicarbonate of soda is used on its own.

Fats

Several sorts of fat can be used in cakes. For purists, butter gives the best possible flavour; however, in my experience, you can now make a very good-flavoured cake with margarine—especially since margarine itself has improved in flavour—so wherever I have suggested butter, block margarine can be used as an alternative. Soft tub margarine is one of the best things that ever happened to cake-making. With it you can make cakes *all-in-one* (provided you add a little extra raising powder)—no creaming, no curdling, just whisk all the ingredients together!

The all-in-one method is not suitable for all cakes, because the mixture tends to be softer and fruit inclines to sink to the bottom (so the flour content needs to be increased to make the cake heavier). But I *do* think it produces the best sponge-cakes of all.

Lard can sometimes be used in cakes (see Marmalade Cake), and the all-in-one process can be used with a whipped white vegetable fat. Do remember, though, that for all recipes except those where the fat is melted, it's important to start with the fat at *room temperature* and not straight from the fridge.

Sugar

Caster sugar dissolves more easily than granulated, and gives a finer texture to most cakes. But as it has become so expensive of late, you might try experimenting with making granulated into caster in a liquidiser. It takes two seconds, but be careful not to overdo it or it will turn into icing sugar! Soft brown sugar and demerara are sometimes called for, especially in wholefood cakes.

Eggs

Eggs to be used in cakes should be at room temperature, as they curdle more easily if they're too cold. I never keep my eggs in the fridge personally, because it's my opinion that too low a temperature spoils them (and certainly doesn't keep them fresh longer). And talking about freshness, bear in mind that shop-bought eggs are never less than seven days old, and after fourteen days they start to go stale and the flavour deteriorates. And while new-laid eggs hot from the nest (or just a day or two old) are actually not as good for cakes as week-old ones, really stale eggs are worse particularly if you have to separate the yolks from the whites! In this book I've found it necessary to use both standard and large eggs (as some mixtures need a fraction more egg than others), but if a mixture using standard eggs seems a little dry, add just a spot of warm water.

Yeast

Yeast cookery has a few pitfalls—so a word or two of warning. First of all I haven't used *fresh yeast* in any of the recipes, because supplies are always so unreliable—and quite honestly, when I have used it I haven't noticed any appreciably better results than with dried. All the same, like fresh yeast, dried yeast can become stale and inactive, and if you buy it in cellophane packets (rather than in sealed airtight tins) it's perfectly possible to get a duff batch.

If it doesn't froth up to a good 'beery' head, it's probably stale and won't raise the mixture. Even with sealed tins be sure to replace the plastic lid tightly after opening, and don't keep it longer than 2 months before using.

Rising mixtures need a warm place, and *no* draughts. I use the warming compartment of my oven. Equally, too high a temperature for a rise can kill off the yeast, and you won't get a proper rise. If a mixture seems slow in rising, don't panic; just give it more time, because if the yeast was okay it will eventually. One final point: if you want to use fresh yeast, remember to use twice the amount you would of dried (i.e. $\frac{1}{2}$ oz of dried = 1 oz of fresh).

PANIC POINTS

Lack of confidence causes panics, and panics cause failures. My job, then, is to build up *your* confidence. On paper that isn't easy, but one thing I must say first of all is don't feel you have to be too much of a perfectionist. I'll admit that a crater, 3 inches wide and 2 inches deep, in the middle of a cake is a bit worrying, and if it really is that bad you probably didn't have the right tin. However, slight imperfections honestly don't matter. Always remember that homemade cakes are full of good things, and if they don't happen to look like first-prize winners they will still *taste* good, and that's what it's really all about. Anyway, here are a few tips on points that sometimes cause panic.

Is it cooked? Basically there are three ways of telling: (i) if it shrinks away slightly from the side of the tin, (ii) if the centre feels springy when lightly touched with the little finger, and (iii) well, I have some reservations about this one. It is the skewer test which goes something like this: if a skewer is inserted in the centre of the cake and comes out clean—the cake is cooked. This is all very well, but if you happen to stick the skewer straight through a cherry, date or other sticky ingredient how can it come out clean? So my advice is to take this into consideration when using the skewer test.

There are other suggestions like 'if you can smell the cake', but I've often been able to smell a cake when it's only half-cooked! Likewise 'if you can hear sizzling noises', but that is equally unreliable. On the whole I plump for the first two methods of telling when a cake is cooked—emphasising once again that ideally you should *leave it alone* and not hike it out to have a look too early on.

Why has it sunk? Often the cause of this problem is related to what was said above, that is, the cake has been tested too soon and the centre dips because it has been touched too early. If however it is the fruit or cherries that have sunk, that usually means the mixture is too slack. All the cakes in this book have been carefully tested to obtain the right balance, so you shouldn't really find this a problem if you follow all the directions carefully.

To sum up on these points, I'd like to say that on the whole what's wrong with a cake is usually more likely to be what's wrong with the recipe. If you follow tried and trusted recipes to the letter, you shouldn't really have any problems. However, if you deviate, then you're on your own!

PRACTICAL POINTS

1 *Preparation of Cake Tins*

Some of my cake tins are coated with a non-stick surface, others are not. However, I've learned *never* to rely on so-called

A Base lining a sponge tin with greaseproof paper.

1.   2.   3.   4.

B Rectangular cake tin

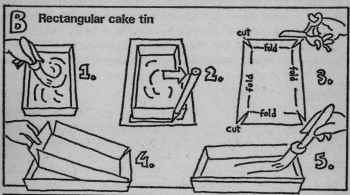

1.   2.   3.
cut — fold — cut
fold   fold
cut — fold
4.   5.

C Deep cake tin
Follow steps 2&3 same as 'A' only cut two rounds of greaseproof paper

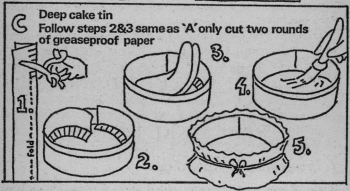

1.   2.   3.   4.   5.

non-stick tins, because they sometimes do. What I strongly recommend is that you ignore this and grease and line all tins in accordance with the instructions in each recipe.

Greasing

I always use the fat that's called for in the recipe for greasing the tin, and I usually apply it with a piece of absorbent kitchen paper (which is softer than the greaseproof and gets into the corners more effectively). Alternatively melted fat can be applied with a brush. A light, even coating is what's needed, neither a great dollop of fat nor a few sketchy flicks. It's been said that salted butter used for greasing can cause the crust to over-bake, but I haven't found this a problem at all (maybe because nowadays commercial butter is not very highly salted).

Flouring

If a recipe states that a cake tin should be greased first and then floured, this is usually because a slightly crisper crust is needed —as in, say, the Madeleines on page 141. Otherwise flouring tins is unnecessary.

Lining tins

Ordinary greaseproof paper is all that's required for lining most tins, except for meringue mixtures where a silicone paper (such as 'Bakewell') is better. When the base of a greased tin is lined with greaseproof it's sometimes necessary to grease the paper as well, to make it easier to peel off after cooking. Rich fruit cakes require a bit more protection as they have to stay in the oven for a longer period—so for these you should tie a double band of brown paper around the outside of the tin. *Note:* the instructions for lining tins are illustrated on page 23.

2 Storing Cakes

Most cakes keep best stored in an airtight tin, and the same with biscuits (but never store both in the same tin or the biscuits will go soggy). However, if no tin is available, use double foil (except for rich fruit cakes, which need longer storing and should be wrapped first in greaseproof and then in foil, as the acid in the fruit can corrode the foil and a mould can develop).

Sponge Cakes

I would imagine that, if a survey were conducted on what was really Britain's national dish, after roast beef and Yorkshire pud then surely Victoria sponge would come a very close second. For as long as there have been fêtes, bazaars and garden parties there have been regiments of Victoria sponges paraded for the envy and admiration of the less-capable. It almost seems that, if half the population can't cook Victoria sponges, the other half cook nothing else!

Personally I've always thought there are plenty more interesting cakes in the world—as I hope you'll gather from the rest of this book. However, if a sponge cake is what you want but fear the skill eludes you, I have only one thing to say to you, and that is *soft margarine*.

Over the last decade margarine has come on a lot in flavour, and nowadays the whipped, soft 'tub' varieties mean that anyone from nine to ninety *can* whip up a sponge cake all-in-one in minutes. Ah! (I can hear the experts saying) but is it the same? I think in some ways it's actually better: it's light, stays moist and keeps beautifully. But to be absolutely fair I invited some friends to a tasting of the all-in-one and the classic Victoria, together with a fatless sponge and the Genoese.

Everyone liked the texture of the all-in-one, but tasted side-by-side the Victoria sandwich (containing butter) did have a slightly better flavour—though how often are they likely to be tasted side-by-side? The Genoese method produces a lovely light sponge but needs a fair amount of skill to prepare: the fatless whisked sponge is light too but the absence of fat can cause dryness and it doesn't keep at all well. In the last analysis it's what *you* personally prefer, so in this chapter I've given a cross-section of methods.

Note on tins: all the sponge cake recipes here are for 7-inch (18 cm) sandwich tins, which is a good average size. However, they must have a proper depth (approx 1½ inches or 4 cm). As I've said, I find non-stick surfaces irrelevant but I do think good-quality solid cake tins are worth paying extra for—I use Tower 7-inch (18 cm) tins which are available at most Woolworth's.

Cake sizes: a lot of pictures of sponge cakes in magazines show too much depth of cake, in my opinion, and a beginner can worry about their sponges not being high enough. With a 4-oz (110 g) mixture you will only get about 1 inch (2·5 cm) of depth on each sponge, but don't forget that when they're sandwiched together the finished cake will be 2 inches (5 cm) excluding the filling; and I think more than that spoils the balance between cake and filling. If you do want to make a deeper sponge cake, still use the 7-inch (18 cm) tin but increase the dry ingredients to 6 oz (75 g) and the eggs to 3 (as in the Lemon Curd Cake) then, to balance the filling, slice each sponge in two, making four layers in all.

Victoria Sponge Cake

The classic way to make a Victoria sponge is to weigh the eggs
on one side of a pair of balance scales (where the weights stand),
and weigh the other ingredients on the scale pan so as to be
absolutely accurate. I have followed this method faithfully, and
found 2 *standard* eggs weigh 4 oz (110 g) but do not provide
enough liquid for the mixture—so I now use 2 large eggs and
weigh everything else in the normal way.

4 oz butter (*must* be room temperature) (110 g)
4 oz caster sugar (110 g)
2 large eggs
4 oz self-raising flour (110 g)
hot water, if needed

To finish: jam
sifted icing sugar

Pre-heat the oven to gas mark 3 (325 °F) (170 °C)

Two 7-inch (18 cm) sponge tins at least 1½ inches (4 cm) deep,
greased and the bases lined with greaseproof paper.

In a medium-sized mixing bowl cream the butter and sugar
together until you get a pale, fluffy mixture that drops off the
spoon easily (an electric hand-whisk speeds this up consider-
ably, but a wooden spoon will do). Then in a separate jug or
bowl, beat the eggs thoroughly together, then add them a little
at a time, beating well after each addition. For a beginner I
would recommend just a teaspoonful of egg at a time: if you
add it like this, just a little at a time and beating after each addition, you'll find the mixture won't curdle. (Why shouldn't it
curdle, you're thinking? Well, some of the hidden air that by
now has been beaten into the mixture will escape if the mixture
'breaks', and as air is what makes a cake light, curdling will
make it slightly heavier.)

When the eggs have been incorporated, take a metal tablespoon, which will cut and fold the flour in much better than a
thick wooden spoon. Have the flour in a sieve resting on a
plate, then lift the sieve high above the bowl and sift about a

quarter of it on to the mixture—then replace the sieve on the plate and lightly and gently fold the flour into the mixture (if you beat the flour in, again you'll lose some precious air). Then repeat this until all the flour is incorporated: lifting the sieve up high above the bowl will ensure the flour gets a good airing before it reaches the mixture.

Now the flour has been added you should have a mixture that will drop off the spoon easily when you tap it on the side of the bowl. If not, add some hot water, one or two teaspoonfuls or if you're using standard eggs you may need a tablespoonful. Now divide the mixture equally between the prepared tins—if you want to be very precise you could place both tins on balance scales (I've never bothered though because, quite honestly, I don't mind if one sponge is fractionally larger than the other). Place them on the centre shelf of the oven, and they'll take about 25–30 minutes to cook. When they are cooked the centres will feel springy when lightly touched with a little finger-tip and no imprint remains. I think the secret of success here is to be patient and not to have crafty peeps halfway through: a sudden rush of cold coming into the oven can cause the cakes to sink.

When they're cooked remove them from the oven, then after about 1 minute turn them out on to a wire cooling tray, loosening them around the edges with a palette knife first. Then carefully peel off the base papers and leave the cakes to cool completely before sandwiching them together with jam and sifting a little icing sugar over the surface. The fillings can vary from just jam or a mixture of jam and whipped cream, to lemon curd (*see* pages 39–40), or chocolate fudge icing (page 87). Also you can flavour the cake mixture with grated lemon or orange rind or a few drops of vanilla essence. For a coffee flavour, dilute a tablespoon of instant coffee with a dessertspoon of hot water. For a chocolate flavour, take out a level tablespoon of flour and replace it with a level tablespoon of cocoa.

Note: For an 8 inch (20 cm) sponge cake use 6 oz (175 g) of each ingredient and 3 eggs.

Genoese Sponge Cake

While the Victoria sponge is universal in England, on the continent the accepted method is the Genoese. It's a much more complicated process, in my opinion, and although the texture is in some ways lighter and more springy—if badly made springiness can border on rubbery-ness. Those are only my personal feelings of course, and I'm including the Genoese recipe for those of you who like to experiment with different methods to find out which you prefer.

3 oz plain flour, sifted (75 g)
1 oz cornflour (25 g)
3 standard eggs
2 oz butter (50 g)
4 oz caster sugar (110 g)

To finish: jam
sifted icing sugar

Pre-heat the oven to gas mark 4 (350 °F) (180 °C)

Two 7-inch (18 cm) sandwich tins (1½ inches [4 cm] deep) greased, and the bases lined with greaseproof paper (also greased).

Begin by sifting the flour on to the scale pan, lifting the sieve high to give the flour an airing. Then place the butter in a small saucepan and allow it to warm and melt (but it mustn't get too hot, so don't leave it unattended). Now place the eggs and sugar in a large mixing bowl, then fit the bowl over a saucepan of very hot, but not simmering, water.

Start to whisk the mixture with an electric hand-whisk until it becomes very thick, foamy and pale-coloured. Then remove it from the heat and continue whisking until it has cooled. Now place a sieve over the bowl and sift half the flour into the mixture. Next sprinkle in the warmed butter and gently fold that in, followed by the rest of the flour—all the time *folding* not beating. While you're folding the mixture will lose some of its volume but that's quite normal, so don't worry. Now divide the mixture evenly between the two prepared tins and bake them on the centre shelf of the oven for 25 minutes, or until springy when lightly touched in the centre. Leave the cakes in the tins for about 1 minute before loosening the edges and turning out on to a wire rack to cool. Carefully peel off the base papers, and sandwich together with jam only when absolutely cold. Dust the top with sifted icing sugar.

Whisked Sponge Cake

This sponge cake doesn't have any fat in it and is, therefore, best eaten as fresh as possible.

3 oz plain flour, sifted (75 g)
½ teaspoon baking powder
3 large eggs
3 oz caster sugar (75 g)

Pre-heat the oven to gas mark 4 (350 °F) (180 °C)

Prepare two 7-inch (18 cm) sandwich tins by brushing liberally with melted fat and lining the bases with greaseproof paper also greased.

Start by separating the eggs and placing the whites in a very large grease-free bowl and the yolks in a separate bowl. Now add the sugar to the yolks and whisk, either by hand or with an electric hand-whisk, until the mixture is thick, very pale and fluffy. (With an electric whisk this takes about 5 minutes.) Then wash and dry the whisk very thoroughly and beat the whites until stiff but not dry. Now, using a large metal spoon, fold the egg whites into the yolks and sugar mixture alternately with the sifted flour and baking powder, starting and finishing with egg whites. Then spoon an equal quantity of the mixture into the prepared tins and bake in the centre of the oven for 20–25 minutes. The cakes should feel firm and springy in the centre and have begun to shrink slightly from the sides of the tins. Leave them to cool in the tins for 3 minutes, then have ready a sheet of greaseproof paper, sprinkled with a little caster sugar.

Turn the cakes out on to this before transferring them to a wire rack to finish cooling. Then sandwich them together with any sort of jam or lemon curd or either of these and fresh cream as well.

All-In-One Sponge

4 oz self-raising flour, sifted (110 g)
1 level teaspoon baking powder
4 oz soft tub margarine (room temperature) (110 g)
4 oz caster sugar (110 g)
2 large eggs
2–3 drops vanilla essence

Pre-heat the oven to gas mark 3 (325 °F) (170 °C)

Two 7-inch (18 cm) sponge tins, lightly buttered and their bases lined with greaseproof paper—these tins should be no less than 1 inch deep.

Combine all the ingredients in a mixing bowl and whisk with an electric hand-whisk for about 1 minute, or until everything is thoroughly mixed. Now divide the mixture between the two prepared tins, level off and bake on the centre shelf of the oven for about 30 minutes. When cooked leave them in the tins for only about 30 seconds before turning them out on to a wire cooling tray.

When cool, sandwich them together with any sort of jam, or lemon curd, or with jam and fresh cream.

Swiss Roll

This is a particularly easy Swiss roll made by the all-in-one method. I find it behaves fairly well and isn't likely to crack but, if it does, it will still taste the same.

2 oz soft margarine (50 g)
4 oz caster sugar (110 g)

2 large eggs
4 oz sifted self-raising flour (110 g)
1 tablespoon hot water
a little extra caster sugar

For the filling:
3–4 tablespoons warmed jam

Pre-heat the oven to gas mark 6 (400 °F) (200 °C)

Begin by preparing a Swiss roll tin, which should measure approximately 8 × 12 inches (20 × 30 cm).

Lightly and thoroughly grease the inside of the tin with melted fat, then line it with enough greaseproof paper to come up half an inch above the sides of the tin. Now brush the greaseproof paper with melted fat (*see* page 22 for information on preparing cake tins).

Place all the ingredients, except the water, in a mixing bowl and mix thoroughly for about 1 minute or until everything is blended. Then add enough hot water to make a dropping consistency—I use about a tablespoonful. Next, spread the mixture evenly in the prepared tin and don't worry if it looks a bit sparse because it will 'puff up' quite a lot. Bake it in the oven for approximately 12 minutes or until it feels springy in the centre.

Whilst it's cooking you can prepare everything for the rolling operation. First of all you need a damp tea towel spread out on a flat surface, then on top of the tea towel you place a sheet of greaseproof paper that's about 1 inch (2·5 cm) larger than the Swiss roll tin. Then sprinkle caster sugar all over the greaseproof paper. At this stage also warm the jam to make it easier to spread.

As soon as the Swiss roll is cooked, loosen round the edges with a palette knife and turn it out on to the greaseproof paper immediately. Now carefully and gently strip off the base paper and spread the cake with the warmed jam. Before you start to roll it, take a sharp knife and trim the barest $\frac{1}{8}$ of an inch (3 mm) from all round the cake. This will make it much neater and help to prevent it from cracking. Now, with one of the shorter edges of the cake nearest to you, make a small incision about 1 inch (2·5 cm) from the edge cutting right across the cake, not too deeply; this will help you when you start to roll. Now start to roll this 1-inch (2·5 cm) piece over and away from you and continue to roll holding the sugared paper behind the cake as you roll the whole thing up. When it's completely rolled up, hold the paper around the cake for a few moments to help it 'set' in position, then transfer the cake to a wire cooling tray.

If you've never made a Swiss roll before, I can assure you this *sounds* much more complicated than it actually is and the whole operation should only take a few minutes. For a chocolate Swiss roll, take out 1 level tablespoon of flour and replace with 1 level tablespoon of cocoa. For a coffee Swiss roll, add 1 tablespoon of instant coffee dissolved with a dessertspoon of hot water to the mixture.

Coffee and Walnut Sponge Cake

This is another easy 'all-in-one' recipe and for anyone who hates the sickly sweetness of butter cream this filling is far lighter, less sweet and much more creamy.

4 oz self-raising flour, sifted twice (110 g)
1 level teaspoon baking powder
4 oz soft margarine (pure vegetable margarine)—must be room temperature (110 g)
4 oz caster sugar (110 g)
2 large eggs
2 oz walnuts, very finely chopped (50 g)
1 tablespoon instant coffee
1 dessertspoon hot water
a little cold water

Pre-heat the oven to gas mark 3 (325 °F) (170 °C)

Two 7-inch (18 cm) sandwich tins approximately 1½ inches (4 cm) deep, lightly greased and with bases lined with greaseproof paper also very lightly greased.

First mix the coffee with a dessertspoon of boiling water so that it dissolves into an essence. Then place all the ingredients, including the coffee essence, in a mixing bowl and mix to a smooth creamy consistency (an electric hand whisk is ideal for this). When you have a good soft dropping consistency, add a teaspoon of cold water and mix that in, then divide the mixture evenly between the two prepared sandwich tins, spreading the mixture around as evenly as you can. Place the tins in the centre of the oven and bake for 30 minutes, by which time the sponges will have risen and be firm and springy to the touch. Take them out, leaving them in the tins only a few seconds before turning them out on to a wire cooling tray. As soon as the sponges are cool sandwich them together with the following mousseline.

Coffee Cream Mousseline

The ingredients for a 7- (18 cm) or 8-inch (20 cm) sponge are:

5 oz unsalted butter (room temperature) (150 g)
2½ oz caster sugar (60 g)
2 large egg yolks
4 tablespoons water
1 tablespoon instant coffee dissolved in 1 tablespoon hot water

For decoration: walnut halves

Place the sugar and water together in a small saucepan and slowly bring it to the boil—keep an eye on it and make sure the sugar has dissolved completely before it comes to the boil. Then let it simmer gently for about 10–15 minutes or until the mixture forms a 'thread' when pressed between thumb and forefinger (to do this take some on a teaspoon, cool it a little, and dip your finger in cold water before testing). If you have a cooking thermometer the temperature should be between 218 °F (103 °C) and 220 °F (105 °C).

Now whisk the egg yolks in a bowl, place the bowl on a damp tea towel to steady it, then pour the sugar syrup on to the egg yolks in a steady stream, whisking all the time. Then whisk the butter in, about 1 oz (50 g) at a time, till you have a smooth fluffy cream. Now whip in the dissolved coffee, and use the cream to sandwich the cake together and to decorate the top. Finally decorate with walnut halves and store the cake in an airtight tin.

Lemon Feather Sponge

This cake is slightly different in that the sponge is made with oil instead of solid fat. I use groundnut oil because it has no flavour, but if you've only got corn oil handy that will do.

5 oz plain flour (150 g)
1 oz cornflour (25 g)
2 level teaspoons baking powder
¼ teaspoon salt
5 oz caster sugar (150 g)
2 standard eggs, separated
3 fl oz plus 1 tablespoon groundnut oil (75 ml)
rind and juice of 1 large lemon

Cake filling and covering:
½ pint whipping cream (275 ml)
4 tablespoons lemon curd (preferably homemade)

Decoration:
angelica 'leaves'

Pre-heat the oven to gas mark 4 (350 °F) (180 °C)

Brush two 7-inch (18 cm) sandwich tins with oil, then line the bases with circles of greaseproof paper and brush the paper with oil as well.

Sift the dry ingredients into a bowl and stir in the sugar. Then in another bowl combine the egg yolks with the oil and 3 fl oz (75 ml) water. Beat this liquid into the dry ingredients to form a smooth batter, adding the lemon juice and rind as well. Then whisk the egg whites until stiff but not dry and carefully fold these into the batter. Then divide the mixture equally between the two prepared tins. Bake them in the centre of the oven for 40 minutes or until the cake has shrunk slightly from the sides of the tins and the centre feels springy. Leave them to cool in the tin for a minute or two then turn them out on to a wire rack, and leave to cool.

To finish off, spread the base of one cake round with 2 table-spoons lemon curd. Then put the rest of it in a bowl with the whipping cream and beat until it thickens. Spread the other cake base with about a third of the cream; sandwich the two rounds together then use the remaining cream to cover the top and sides of the cake, smoothing it over evenly with a palette knife. Finally, using a large knife, make a pattern on top of the cake, dividing it into eight sections, then decorate each section with angelica cut into diamond shapes like 'leaves'.

Fresh Lemon Curd Cake

This cake is very light, very fresh and lemony, and altogether quite delicious.

6 oz self-raising flour, sifted (175 g)
1 level teaspoon baking powder
6 oz soft margarine (175 g)
6 oz caster sugar (175 g)
3 standard eggs
grated rind of a lemon
1 tablespoon lemon juice

And for the lemon curd:
3 oz caster sugar (75 g)
1 large juicy lemon (grated rind and juice)
2 large eggs
2 oz unsalted butter (50 g)

icing sugar to decorate

Pre-heat the oven to gas mark 3 (325 °F) (170 °C)

Prepare two 7-inch (18 cm) sandwich tins 1½ inches (4 cm) deep by greasing them, lining the bases with greaseproof paper and greasing that lightly too.

Just measure *all* the cake ingredients into a mixing bowl and beat—ideally with an electric hand-whisk—till you have a smooth creamy consistency. Then divide the mixture evenly between the two tins and bake them on the centre shelf of the oven for about 35 minutes or until the centres spring when lightly touched with a little finger. Turn them out on to a wire cooling tray after about 30 seconds from the oven. When they are absolutely cold—and not before—carefully cut each one horizontally into two with a good sharp serrated knife. Now make the lemon curd—place the grated lemon rind and sugar in a bowl, whisk the lemon juice together with the eggs, then pour this over the sugar. Then add the butter cut into little pieces, and place the bowl over a pan of barely simmering water. Stir frequently till thickened—about 20 minutes. Then cool the curd and use it to sandwich the sponges together, spreading it thickly. Dust the top of the cake with icing sugar and store in an airtight tin.

Chocolate Almond Sponge Cake

This cake looks and tastes very good with some lightly toasted almonds on top, but be very careful as you toast them—one absent-minded glance in another direction and they'll burn!

4 oz self-raising flour (sifted twice) (110 g)
1 teaspoon baking powder
4 oz soft margarine (110 g)
4 oz dark soft brown sugar (110 g)
2 large eggs
2 oz ground almonds (50 g)
1 tablespoon cocoa powder mixed with 1 dessertspoon hot water

Then for the filling and topping:
8 oz plain chocolate (225 g)
1 tablespoon water
1 oz flaked almonds, light toasted (25 g)

Pre-heat the oven to gas mark 3 (325 °F) (170 °C)

For this you'll need to have two 7-inch (18 cm) sandwich tins 1 inch (2·5 cm) in depth. Grease them thoroughly and line the bases with greaseproof paper (also greased).

To make the sponges, place all the ingredients in a bowl, then whisk with an electric whisk (or beat by hand) for about 1 minute or until everything is very thoroughly blended. Then divide the mixture between the two prepared tins, even them out, and bake in the centre of the oven for about 30 minutes. Turn them out after a few seconds on to a wire rack to cool, peeling off the paper. Then melt the chocolate and water together in a double saucepan, and use this to sandwich the cakes and to spread on top. Then sprinkle with toasted almonds, and store the cake in an airtight tin.

Lemon Griessetorte

This cake is made with a mixture of ground almonds and fine semolina, which gives it an unusual but very light texture.

4 oz caster sugar (110 g)
3 large eggs, separated
½ oz ground almonds (10 g)
2 oz semolina (50 g)
grated rind and juice of ½ a large lemon
4 tablespoons lemon curd (*see* page 39)
¼ pint double cream, whipped (150 ml)
icing sugar

Pre-heat the oven to gas mark 4 (350 °F) (180 °C)

One 7-inch (18 cm) round cake tin, greased and the base lined with greaseproof paper also lightly greased.

After separating the eggs, place the yolks into a mixing bowl, then add the sugar and lemon juice and whisk until the mixture is thick and beginning to turn pale. Now stir in the lemon rind, semolina and ground almonds, mixing well to blend everything evenly. Next, using a grease-free whisk and a clean bowl, whisk the egg whites to the soft peak stage. Now take a metal spoon and very carefully and gently fold them into the egg yolk mixture. Pour the cake mix into the prepared tin and bake it in the centre of the oven for about 40 to 50 minutes or until it feels firm and springy in the centre. Let the cake cool in the tin for 10 minutes, then turn it out on to a cooling tray. When it's cold split it in half, then spread both halves with lemon curd and whipped cream. Sandwich them together again and dust with a little icing sugar.

Loaf Cakes
Tea Breads
Etc.

What is a poor cookery writer to do with loaf cakes when there are so many different *sizes* of loaf tin about? I counted fifteen different sizes in one kitchen shop. Which size to opt for in this book has caused me quite a few headaches, I can tell you. With cakes the size of the tin really does matter, and if a recipe calls for one 9 × 5 × 3 it is so infuriating if *you* only have an 8 × 4 × 2. If a recipe says bake in a large or small loaf tin, as some old cookery books do, beware, because in those days there may only have been one or two sizes. Now it's got all very confusing—I don't want to raise the unemployment figures further but there are already too many sizes to cope with, and I dread to think what further confusion the change-over to metric will bring.

I decided, after much thought, to use mostly old-fashioned bread tins which, unlike ordinary loaf tins, have pleated corners, rims and double bases. This is partly as an economy measure because we can all make our bread and cakes in the same tins, and partly to avoid confusion since bread tins come in two sizes, 2 lb (900 g) and 1 lb (450 g). The inside top measurements of the 2 lb size are 7¼ inches (18·5 cm) by 4½ (11·5 cm) and the depth 3¼ inches (8·5 cm); the 1 lb size is 6 inches (15 cm) by 3¾ (9·5 cm) and 2¾ inches (7 cm) deep. (If you have any problems locating these tins, David Mellor Ironmongers, 4 Sloane Square, London SW1, tel: 01-730-4259, stock them and offer a mail-order service.) I also find these tins very solid and, provided they are well greased, no linings are necessary. However, just to be on the safe side, I have satisfactorily listed all the loaf-cake recipes in an alternative tin. This is made by Skyline and has a base measuring 7½ inches (19 cm) by 3½ (8·5 cm). So you can use either.

Bara Brith

In Welsh Bara Brith means speckled bread. There are very many versions, some without yeast rather like the sultana loaf on page 53. However, in my Welsh childhood I remember it made with yeast, very spicy and spread with lots of butter.

1 lb strong plain flour (450 g)
4 teaspoons dried yeast
8 fl oz milk (225 ml)
2 oz brown sugar (50 g) *plus* 1 teaspoon
1 teaspoon salt
3 oz butter or margarine (75 g)
1 standard egg
1 teaspoon mixed spice
12 oz mixed dried fruit (350 g)

A 2-lb (900 g) loaf tin well greased

First warm the milk in a small saucepan till it's hand-hot, and then pour it into a bowl. Whisk in 1 teaspoon of sugar, followed by the yeast, then leave it aside in a warm place to froth for about 15 minutes. Now sift the flour and salt into a large mixing bowl, stirring in the sugar as well.

Then rub the fat into the dry ingredients until the mixture looks like fine breadcrumbs. Stir in the mixed spice next, then pour in the beaten egg and frothed yeast, and mix to a dough. Now turn the dough on to a floured surface and knead until smooth and elastic (about 10 minutes), then replace the dough in the bowl and cover with a cloth or some clingfilm. Leave in a warm place to rise until it has doubled in size—about 1½ hours.

After that turn the dough out and knock it down to get the air out, then gradually knead the fruit in and pat out to a rectangular shape. Roll it up from one short side to the other and put in the loaf tin (seam-side down). Place the tin inside an oiled plastic bag and leave it to rise, until the dough has rounded nicely above the edge of the tin (about 30–45 minutes). Meanwhile pre-heat the oven to gas mark 5 (375 °F) (190 °C).

When the dough has risen and springs back when pressed

lightly with a floured finger, remove the polythene bag and transfer the loaf to the oven and bake on the shelf below centre for 30 minutes. Then cover the top of the loaf tin with foil to prevent it overbrowning, and continue to bake for a further 30 minutes. Turn the loaf out, holding it in a teacloth in one hand and tapping the base with the other. It should sound hollow— if not pop it back upside down (without the tin) for five more minutes. Cool the loaf on a wire rack, and brush the top with clear honey, to make it nice and sticky, before the loaf cools. Slice thinly and serve buttered.

Old-Fashioned Lardy Cake

Lardy cake is rather like a huge spicy fruit bun.

For the dough:
1 lb plain flour (450 g)
2 level teaspoons salt
½ oz lard (10 g)
1 teaspoon sugar
2 teaspoons dried yeast
½ pint warm (hand hot) water (275 ml)

For the filling:
5 oz pure English lard (150 g)
4 oz brown sugar (110 g)
½ teaspoon mixed spice
3 oz currants (75 g)
3 oz sultanas (75 g)

Pre-heat the oven to gas mark 6 (400 °F) (200 °C)

Grease an ordinary roasting tin, approximately 8 × 11 inches (20 × 28 cm).

Start by dissolving the sugar in the warm water, sprinkling the dried yeast in, stirring with a fork and leaving it for about 10 minutes until it has a good frothy head on it. While that's happening, sift the flour into a bowl with the salt and rub the lard into it, then pour in the frothy yeast liquid and stir and

46

mix to a dough. Now transfer the dough to a working surface and knead it for about 10 minutes until it becomes smooth and elastic. Put the dough back into the bowl, then cover the whole thing including the bowl with a large polythene bag (a pedal bin liner is ideal), and secure it to seal. Now leave the dough to rise—it should take about 2 hours at ordinary kitchen temperature or only 1 hour if it's in a warm place. When it's doubled in size, turn it out on to a lightly floured surface and roll it into a long strip, about three times as long as it's wide.

Now for the filling dot a third of the lard in little pats all over the dough. In a small bowl mix the sugar, spice and fruit together, then sprinkle a third of this all along the dough. Now roll it up into a roll, then give it a quarter turn, placing the seam underneath, seal each end of the roll by giving it a sharp tap with a rolling pin so that you trap in the air. Now roll it out again and repeat the lard, sugar and rolling process twice more. Finally, roll the dough out to an oblong that will fit the tin. Then take a sharp knife and score the top of the dough across and across as if you were scoring pork rind. Now place the tin inside the polythene bag again, seal, and leave it in a warm place until it's doubled in size once more. Remove the polythene bag, then bake the lardy cake for about 30 minutes until it's golden brown and risen in the centre. Leave it in the tin for 10 minutes to cool and brush it with a glaze made by dissolving 1 tablespoon of sugar in 1 tablespoon of water. Then turn it out of the tin and serve cut in thick slices.

Sticky Date Cake

This cake has no eggs or sugar in it—it's made with condensed milk, which gives it a lovely dark toffee flavour.

4 oz raisins (110 g)
8 oz chopped dates (225 g)
6 oz sultanas (175 g)
4 oz currants (110 g)
10 oz margarine (275 g)
½ pint water (275 ml)
1 large-size tin condensed milk
5 oz plain flour (150 g)
5 oz wholemeal flour (150 g)
¾ teaspoon bicarbonate of soda
a pinch of salt
1 tablespoon chunky marmalade

Pre-heat the oven to gas mark 3 (325 °F) (170 °C)

You'll need an 8-inch (20 cm) cake tin lined with greaseproof paper.

Begin by placing all the fruits, the margarine, water and condensed milk in a saucepan, then simply bring it to the boil, stirring quite frequently to prevent it sticking. Let the mixture simmer for 3 minutes exactly—still stirring occasionally and, whatever you do, don't forget it. Now transfer the mixture to a large mixing bowl, to cool off for about 30 minutes. While it's cooling, weigh out the flour, then sift it on to a plate, adding the salt and bircarbonate of soda. (When you sieve wholemeal flour there's usually some bits of bran left in the sieve, so just tip it back on to the rest of the sieved flour.) When the fruit mixture has cooled, stir the flour, salt and bicarbonate of soda into it, adding a nice round tablespoon of marmalade too. Then spoon the mixture into the prepared tin and bake the cake on the centre shelf of the oven for 2½–3 hours. Have a look halfway through, and if the top of the cake looks a bit dark put a double square of greaseproof on top to protect it. Then let the cake cool in the tin for 5 minutes before turning it out to cool on a wire tray. This is quite a large cake—but fear not, it keeps for several weeks in an airtight tin and, I think, actually improves with keeping.

Irish Tea Cake

This tastes lovely when freshly made—served cut in thick slices well buttered. It also keeps very well but you'll have to remember always to start it off the night before you need it.

½ pint strong cold tea (275 ml)
1 lb dried mixed fruits (Sainsburys are good) (450 g)
8 oz demerara sugar (225 g)
4 oz walnuts, chopped (110 g)
4 oz glacé cherries, rinsed, dried and quartered (110 g)
1 large egg, beaten together with 2 tablespoons milk
1 lb self-raising flour (450 g)

Prepare the fruit by soaking it with the sugar in the cold tea overnight. Then the next day simply stir in all the remaining ingredients, and spread the mixture into a very well-greased roasting tin measuring 11½ × 9 inches (29 × 23 cm). Bake in the centre of a pre-heated oven, gas mark 3 (325 °F) (170 °C) for about an hour and ten minutes or until golden brown on top and springy to touch in the centre. Then straight away turn it out on to a wire rack, turning it the right way up again. As soon as it's cool slice across into about ½-inch (1 cm) thick slices and serve thickly spread with butter.

Note: You don't need to line the tin for this recipe.

Sticky Malt Loaf   (Makes 2 small loaves)

This, being a very rich yeast dough, takes a long time to rise but, provided you're not in a hurry, is very simple.

1 lb plain flour (450 g)
8 fl oz hand-hot water (225 ml)
1 teaspoon salt
8 oz sultanas (225 g)
1 teaspoon brown sugar
1 tablespoon dried yeast
4 tablespoons malt extract
2 tablespoons black treacle
1 oz butter or margarine (25 g)
Honey or golden syrup to glaze

No pre-heating temperature because it's not needed till much later!

Two 1-lb loaf tins (450 g) brushed with melted fat.

First sift the flour and salt into a bowl and stir in the sultanas. Then put the sugar into a glass measuring jug and pour in 8 fl oz (225 ml) warm water. Stir well then sprinkle in the yeast. Whisk lightly with a fork and leave the mixture to froth for about 10–15 minutes. Now combine the malt extract, treacle and fat together in a small saucepan and heat gently until the fat melts. Then take the pan from the heat and leave it until it's just warm. Next pour the frothed yeast and barely warm syrup mixture on to the flour and mix very thoroughly to a soft, sticky, dough. Now spoon an equal quantity of the mix into the prepared tins. Level off the mixture, using the back of a spoon, or the back of your hand. Place the tins in a large, oiled plastic bag. Trap a little air in the bag so it balloons up and the plastic is not in contact with the top of the tins. Then seal the bag and leave in a warm place to rise to the top of the tins. This can take between 2–5 hours, depending on the warmth. Then bake the loaves at mark 5 (375 °F) (190 °C) for 40 minutes. Turn the loaves out of the tins and tap the bases— they should sound hollow. If not, return them to the oven upside down without the tins for a further 5 minutes. Then brush the loaves with honey or golden syrup and leave them to cool on a wire rack before slicing and buttering.

Note: When making two loaves, as in the above recipe, the easiest way to make sure you have the same amount of mixture in both tins is to place both the tins on balance scales—one where the weights should normally go and one on the scale pan—then you can balance the mixture perfectly.

Moll's Marmalade Cake

This cake has a superb flavour and cuts even better after a couple of days' storing. Moll, who gave me this recipe, says not to worry if it dips slightly in the centre. Its superb flavour will make up for that.

8 oz self-raising flour, sifted (225 g)
4 oz sugar (110 g)
2 oz butter (room temperature) (50 g)
2 oz lard (room temperature) (50 g)
1 rounded tablespoon thick marmalade
grated rind of ½ a large lemon
grated rind of ½ a large orange
1 teaspoon mixed spice
1 teaspoon vinegar
pinch of salt
6 fl oz milk (170 ml)
4 oz mixed dried fruit (110 g)

For the topping:
1 tablespoon demerara sugar

Pre-heat the oven to gas mark 4 (350 °F) (180 °C)

This cake is best made in a Skyline loaf tin 7½ × 3½ inches base measurement (19 cm × 8·5 cm) greased and base lined with lightly greased greaseproof paper.

Begin by rubbing the butter and lard into the flour until crumbly, then add the sugar, salt, mixed fruit, spice, lemon and orange rinds. Stir in the milk a little at a time and the vinegar and mix until the ingredients are distributed evenly. Now stir in the marmalade and you should have a good dropping consistency, so that if you tap a spoonful of the mixture on the side of the bowl it drops off easily. Then spoon the mixture into the prepared tin, spreading it out evenly. Now sprinkle the surface with the demerara sugar and bake for 1–1¼ hours. When its cooked the cake will have shrunk away from the side of the tin and the centre will be firm and springy. Cool the cake on a wire rack and store in an airtight tin. This is better after a couple of days' keeping.

Dark Jamaican Gingerbread

If you've got two lots of syrup to measure out, the easiest way is to warm the tins first then measure in glass measuring jugs.

¾ lb plain flour, sifted (350 g)
6 oz butter (175 g)
1½ teaspoons ground ginger
2 level teaspoons ground cinnamon
⅛ of a nutmeg, grated
1 level teaspoon bicarbonate of soda
4 tablespoons milk
6 oz black treacle (175 g)
6 oz golden syrup (175 g)
6 oz dark soft brown sugar (175 g)
2 eggs, lightly beaten

Pre-heat the oven to gas mark 3 (325 °F) (170 °C)

Line a buttered 2-lb (900 g) loaf tin with greaseproof paper and paint the paper with a little melted butter as well.

Sift the flour and spices into a large bowl, mix the bicarbonate of soda with the milk and set it on one side. Now measure the black treacle, golden syrup, sugar and butter into a saucepan with ¼ pint (150 ml) of water, heat and gently stir until thoroughly melted and blended but *don't* let it come anywhere near the boil and don't go off and leave it! Next add the

52

syrup mixture to the flour and spices, beating vigorously with a wooden spoon; when the mixture is smooth, beat in the eggs a little at a time, followed by the bicarbonate of soda and milk. Now pour the mixture into the prepared tin and bake in the centre of the oven for $1\frac{1}{4}$–$1\frac{1}{2}$ hours until it's well risen, firm to the touch and has shrunk away slightly from the sides of the tin. Remove the cake from the oven and allow to cool in the tin for 5 minutes before turning out. If possible, leave it in a cake tin for 24 hours before eating, and serve it cut in thick slices spread with butter.

Note: This mixture is too much for the alternative size loaf tin.

Sultana Loaf Cake

This is such a simple little recipe that a child could very easily make it and if, once made, you can possibly bear to wait, you'll find it improves with two days' keeping.

8 oz wholewheat self-raising flour (or white self-raising flour) (225 g)
6 oz demerara sugar (175 g)
6 fl oz cold tea (175 g)
8 oz sultanas (225 g)
1 egg (large)
pinch of salt

Pre-heat the oven to gas mark 4 (350 °F) (180 °C) twenty minutes before baking time

A very well greased 2-lb (900 g) loaf tin.

Begin by placing the sultanas in a basin and pouring the cold tea on them, then leave them to soak for about five hours or, preferably, overnight. After soaking the sultanas will have become large, plump and juicy. Then simply stir the flour, salt and sugar into the sultana mixture. Beat the egg and stir this in too. Don't worry about the absence of fat in this recipe because with the high fruit content it does end up a very moist cake.

Now spoon the mixture into the prepared tin, spread it out evenly and bake the cake on the middle shelf of the oven for about 1 hour. Then leave it in the tin for 10–15 minutes before turning out. Cool and store in a tin till needed and serve in slices spread with butter.

Spiced Date and Walnut Loaf

I have to admit I had three attempts at this cake before I got exactly what I wanted—a dark, rather sticky Date and Walnut Loaf and I think you'll agree that this one is just right.

4 oz margarine (110 g)
6 oz golden syrup (175 g)
2 oz black treacle (50 g)
¼ pint milk (150 ml)
2 large eggs
8 oz plain flour (225 g)
1 teaspoon mixed spice
2 teaspoons ground ginger
1 level teaspoon bicarbonate of soda
4 oz stoned dates (110 g)
2 oz walnuts (50 g)

Pre-heat the oven to gas mark 2 (300 °F) (150 °C)

A 2-lb (900 g) loaf tin, well greased.

First prepare the dates and walnuts. The nuts should be chopped fairly small and, if the dates are cooking dates bought in a block, they should be separated out and then individually chopped into fairly small pieces. If you try to chop them all together they tend to stick and it's hard to separate the pieces out.

Now to make the cake mixture, place the margarine, black treacle and syrup in a large saucepan and melt them together over a gentle heat. Then remove the mixture from the heat, let it cool for a few minutes, then mix the milk into it. Now beat the eggs and add those to the syrup mixture as well. Next, sift

54

the flour, spices and bicarbonate of soda into a bowl and gradually whisk the syrup mixture into the dry ingredients, bit by bit, until you have a smooth batter. Then lightly fold in the walnuts and about two-thirds of the dates, and pour the mixture into the prepared tin. Now lightly drop the rest of the dates on the top, pushing them gently in with a skewer. I find adding this amount of dates last of all gives a better distribution as the mixture is a fairly slack one. Place the cake on the centre shelf of the oven and bake it for 1½ hours to 1 hour 50 minutes by which time it will have a very rounded, slightly cracked top. Cool it in the tin for about half an hour before turning it out. Then when it's absolutely cold, keep it in a tin and, once again, this is a cake that does seem to improve if kept a couple of days before eating.

Banana and Walnut Loaf

I always think this is a good cake for eating out of doors, or taking on a picnic, as the bananas give it a very pronounced flavour.

1½ oz butter (40 g)
1½ oz lard (40 g)
4 oz caster sugar (110 g)
1 egg, beaten
the grated rind of 1 orange and 1 lemon
8 oz plain flour (225 g)
2 level teaspoons baking powder
4 medium bananas peeled
2 oz walnuts roughly chopped (50 g)

Pre-heat the oven to gas mark 4 (350 °F) (180 °C)

For this you'll need a 7½ × 3½ inch (base measurement) loaf tin (19 × 8·5 cm), well buttered.

Cream the butter and lard with the sugar till light and fluffy, then beat in the beaten egg a little at a time, and when that's in add the grated rinds. Now sift the flour and baking powder, and carefully fold it into the creamed mixture using a metal spoon. Then in a separate bowl mash the bananas to a pulp with a large fork, then fold them into the cake mixture together with the chopped walnuts. Now spoon the cake mixture into the prepared tin, level it off on top, and bake for approximately 50–55 minutes. Leave the cake in the tin for 10 minutes then turn it out on to a wire cooling rack. Store in a tin.

Damp Gingerbread

This is a deliciously light textured gingerbread and so moist it stores very well.

12 oz golden syrup (350 g)
4½ oz margarine (125 g)
9 oz plain flour, sifted (250 g)
½ teaspoon salt
1¾ teaspoons bicarbonate of soda
2 teaspoons ground ginger
½ teaspoon mixed spice
1 large egg
½ pint milk (275 ml)

Pre-heat the oven to gas mark 4 (350 °F) (180 °C)

To make this you'll need a tin measuring 7 × 11 × 1½ inches (18 × 28 × 4 cm).

First grease a tin thoroughly (even if it's non-stick) and line the base with greaseproof paper—and grease that too. Now weigh the syrup (by first weighing a small saucepan then pouring in the syrup until you have 12 oz [350 g] above the saucepan's weight). Then add the margarine to the saucepan and melt the two together over a gentle heat until the margarine has melted. Meanwhile measure the dry ingredients into a bowl, then gradually pour on the syrup mixture, mixing thoroughly. When all that's in, beat the egg and milk together in a separate basin then add that bit by bit, again mixing very thoroughly. The cake batter will seem very liquid but that's quite normal—so don't worry, just pour it into the prepared tin and bake in the centre of the oven for about 50 minutes or until the centre is springy. Cool in the tin for 5 minutes before turning out on to a wire tray to cool. When it's cold cut it into squares and store in a tin.

Family Cakes

Unfortunately cakes don't always lend themselves to neat classification, so this chapter covers a rather wide cross-section —at least these are the cakes which are firm favourites in *our* family, which itself is a pretty large cross-section!

For a large family I can recommend the Family Slab Cake, which is made in a meat roasting tin, has a delicious flavour and goes a long way. The Children's Cake is a very easy melted butter sponge mixture, also made in a large square tin—this one offers all sorts of variations, because you can ice sections of it in different colours and then decorate the cut-up squares with all kinds of goodies for a children's party, or if you need plenty of cake around for unexpected tea-time guests in the school holidays—just ice it with plain lemon icing and sprinkle with coconut.

Boil and Bake Cake travels particularly well, and I think is a good choice for taking on a self-catering holiday. For rather special family occasions the Preserved Ginger Cake is out of this world, although the Iced English Walnut Cake gets plenty of votes as well.

Fruit Slab Cake

This is a very simple family cake, with a very good flavour, baked in a meat tin and served cut into squares.

8 oz butter or margarine (room temperature) (225 g)
8 oz caster sugar (225 g)
4 large eggs
a few drops of pure almond essence
10 oz self-raising flour (275 g)
4 oz mixed dried fruit (110 g)
2 oz flaked almonds (50 g)
1 oz glacé cherries, sliced (25 g)
1½ tablespoons granulated sugar

Pre-heat the oven to gas mark 4 (350 °F) (180 °C)

A meat roasting tin measuring approximately 10 × 8 inches (25·5 × 20 cm) and 2 inches (5 cm) deep, well buttered.

Begin by creaming the butter and sugar till fluffy and pale, then beat the eggs and add them a little at a time, beating well after each addition to prevent the mixture curdling. When all the egg has been incorporated, add 3 or 4 drops of almond essence and beat again. Then lightly and carefully fold in the sifted flour—about a tablespoon at a time—and, lastly, fold in the dried fruit and cherries. Now spoon the mixture into the prepared tin, spreading it out evenly, then sprinkle the surface of the cake with the granulated sugar and flaked almonds and bake on the centre shelf of the oven for about 45–55 minutes or until the centre feels springy to the touch. Leave in the tin to cool for 10 minutes before turning out.

Mrs. Gordon's Boil and Bake Cake

I have an aunt who always bakes delicious cakes and this is one of them. It's very easy to make so I would recommend it as a good cake for a beginner.

12 oz mixed dried fruit (350 g)
4 oz any margarine (110 g)
4 oz brown sugar (110 g)
8 oz self-raising flour (225 g)
¼ pint water (150 ml)
2 standard eggs
1 level teaspoon mixed spice

Pre-heat the oven to gas mark 3 (325 °F) (170 °C)

All you do is place the fruit, margarine, sugar and water in a saucepan, then stir it all and bring the mixture up to simmering point. Then simmer it for 20 minutes—keeping the heat fairly low and stirring several times to prevent the mixture from sticking. Don't go away or forget it or it will boil to toffee! After that remove the saucepan from the heat and allow the mixture to cool a bit (about half an hour), then add the sifted flour, mixed spice and the beaten eggs. Mix all this thoroughly, then pour the mixture into a prepared, greased and lined 7-inch (18 cm) cake tin, and bake on the centre shelf of the oven for 30 minutes. Then reduce the heat to gas mark 2 (300 °F) (150 °C) and continue to bake for a further 1½ hours. Allow the cake to cool in the tin for about 10–15 minutes before turning it out to cool on a wire rack. This is a very good cake for storing, as it keeps well in an airtight tin.

Preserved Ginger Cake

This, without doubt, is one of my very favourite cakes, and I'm quite confident that once you've made it you'll love it every bit as much as I do.

6 oz butter (or margarine) at room temperature (175 g)
6 oz caster sugar (175 g)
3 eggs at room temperature
8 oz self-raising flour (225 g)
2 tablespoons ginger syrup (from preserved ginger)
1 tablespoon black treacle
2 teaspoons ground ginger

62

1 tablespoon ground almonds
2 tablespoons milk
6 pieces preserved ginger

For the icing:
4 oz icing sugar, sieved (110 g)
juice of ½ a lemon

Pre-heat the oven to gas mark 3 (325 °F) (170 °C)

Grease and line a tin 11 × 7¼ × 1¼ inches (28 × 18·5 × 3 cm) (slightly deeper than a Swiss roll tin) with greaseproof paper— and grease the paper. Make sure the paper comes about an inch above the edge of the tin.

Place the tin of black treacle in a saucepan of barely simmering water to warm it and make it easier to measure. Then in a large mixing bowl cream the butter and sugar together until light and fluffy. Then break the eggs into a basin and beat them until frothy with a fork, then gradually beat them into the creamed mixture a little at a time, adding about a tablespoon of the measured flour as you get towards beating in the last of the egg. Stir in the ginger syrup and black treacle, and fold in the remaining flour, ground ginger and almonds, followed by the milk. Then chop five of the pieces of stem ginger and fold these into the cake mix too. Spread the cake mix in the tin, then bake for 45–50 minutes or until the cake is risen, springy and firm to the touch in the centre, and has begun to shrink away from the sides of the tin. Leave to cool in the tin for 10 minutes, then turn out on to a wire rack and leave until cold. For the icing, sift the icing sugar into a bowl and mix with the lemon juice and about a teaspoon of water—you will need it about the consistency of thin cream. Spread the icing over the top of the cake, and never mind if it dribbles down the side in a few places—it looks nice and homemade. Cut the remaining piece of stem ginger into fifteen small pieces and arrange in lines of three across the cake. For serving, cut the cake into fifteen pieces, each section with a piece of ginger—delicious.

Iced English Walnut Cake

There are certain cakes which are very English in character and this is one of them—perfect for every sort of cake occasion.

8 oz self-raising flour (225 g)
2 teaspoons baking powder
8 oz soft margarine (room temperature) (225 g)
8 oz caster sugar (225 g)
4 large eggs
3 oz walnuts, finely chopped (75 g)

Filling:
2 oz walnuts, finely chopped (50 g)

Icing:
11 oz granulated sugar (315 g)
4 tablespoons water
2 egg whites
¼ teaspoon cream of tartar
vanilla essence

to decorate: 9 walnut halves

Pre-heat the oven to gas mark 3 (325 °F) (170 °C)

3 × 8-inch (20 cm) sandwich tins greased and base lined with greaseproof paper also greased.

To make the cake put all the ingredients together in a large bowl and beat until thoroughly combined, then spread an equal quantity of the mixture in each of the prepared sandwich tins. Now bake them near the centre of the oven for 30 minutes or until the cakes feel springy in the centre when lightly pressed. Then leave them for 3 or 4 minutes to cool before turning them out on to a cooling rack and stripping off the base papers. When the cake rounds are cold, prepare the icing. Put all the ingredients in a large heat-proof bowl. Then heat a large saucepan containing about 1 inch (2·5 cm) boiling water. Fit the bowl over the boiling water and start to whisk—timing yourself for 7 minutes. (The best type of whisk to use is either a rotary whisk or electric hand whisk.) After 7 minutes remove the bowl from the heat and continue to beat until the icing has a similar consistency to that of softly whipped cream, i.e. it will hold a shape, but not a stiff peak. Now remove a third of the icing to a bowl and combine it with the chopped walnuts and spread this as a filling on two cake rounds before sandwiching the three together. Then continue to beat the rest of the icing until it cools and stiffens slightly. Now slap the icing all over the cake, finishing with a circular swirling movement to give an attractive finish. Top with the walnuts, eight around the edge and the ninth in the centre. Then leave the cake in a cool, dry place to become firm—about 4 hours.

This type of cake frosting will become faintly crisp on the outside but stay soft and fluffy underneath.

Traditional Dundee Cake

If you've never made a Dundee cake it's worth bearing in mind that the texture is light and crumbly, not dark and moist like some of the shop-bought versions. It also tastes better after a week's keeping.

5 oz butter (room temperature) (150 g)
5 oz caster sugar (150 g)
3 large eggs
8 oz plain flour, sifted (225 g)
1 level teaspoon baking powder
6 oz currants (175 g)
6 oz sultanas (175 g)
2 oz glacé cherries, rinsed, dried, and cut into halves (50 g)
2 oz mixed candied peel, finely chopped (50 g)
2 level tablespoons ground almonds
the grated rind of 1 small orange and 1 small lemon
2 oz whole blanched almonds (50 g)

Pre-heat the oven to gas mark 3 (325 °F) (170 °C)

First grease a 7- or 8-inch (18 or 20 cm) round cake tin and line with greaseproof paper.

Put the butter into a mixing bowl. Add the sugar and beat with a wooden spoon until the mixture is light and fluffy (if you have an electric mixer for this, so much the better).

Now whisk the eggs separately and beat the egg mixture into the creamed butter and sugar, a little at a time. When all the egg mixture is beaten in, take a large tablespoon and carefully *fold* in the sifted flour and baking powder. When this is done the mixture should be of a good soft dropping consistency. If it seems too dry, add a dessertspoon of milk. Next carefully fold in all the other ingredients: currants, sultanas, cherries, mixed peel, ground almonds and orange and lemon rind. Now spoon the mixture into the prepared cake tin, spreading it out evenly with the back of the spoon. Then, carefully, arrange the whole almonds in circles all over the top—but drop them on very lightly: if you press them down too hard they will disappear during the cooking. Place the cake in the centre of the oven and bake for 2–2½ hours or until the centre is firm and springy to touch. Allow it to cool before taking it out of the tin. Dundee cake keeps very well in an airtight tin and tastes better if it's kept a few days before cutting.

Spiced Apple and Cider Cake

This can be served cold as a cake or warm, with cream, as a sweet course. Either way it's very good.

5 oz margarine or butter (150 g)
5 oz caster sugar (150 g)
2 standard eggs, beaten
8 oz plain flour (225 g)
1 teaspoon baking powder
1 teaspoon grated nutmeg
¼ pint dry cider (150 ml)
3 smallish cooking apples

For the topping:
1 oz butter (25 g)
1 oz plain flour (25 g)
2 oz dark, soft brown sugar (50 g)
2 teaspoons cinnamon
1 oz blanched almonds, chopped (25 g)

Pre-heat the oven to gas mark 4 (350 °F) (180 °C)

First brush a deep 8-inch (20 cm) loose based cake tin with melted fat. Line the base and sides with greaseproof paper; brush the paper with melted fat too.

Then cream the butter and sugar together until light, pale and fluffy, before adding the eggs a little at a time, beating well between each addition. Now sieve the flour, baking powder and nutmeg on to a sheet of greaseproof paper. Fold half of this into the creamed mix, using a large metal spoon, followed by half the cider, then fold in the rest of the flour etc and, finally, the last of the cider. Now peel, core and chop one of the apples and fold this carefully into the cake mix. Spoon it into the prepared tin then level the top with back of the spoon.

To prepare the topping, measure the butter, flour, sugar and cinnamon into a bowl. Rub the mixture with the finger tips until you have a fairly coarse, crumbly mixture, then add the chopped almonds. Now, quickly, quarter, core and peel the remaining two apples. Slice them thinly and arrange the slices, slightly overlapping, in three circles on top of the cake. Then sprinkle the topping over the apples and bake the cake on the centre shelf for 1½–1¾ hours or until the cake shows signs of shrinking away from the side of the tin. Leave it to cool in the tin for 10 minutes before removing carefully and transferring to a wire rack.

Old-fashioned Cherry Cake

Cherry cake has always been a firm family favourite. However, sometimes without there being any possible explanation those unobliging cherries refuse to stay suspended in the cake and, sadly, end up in a heap at the bottom! To avoid this, rinse the syrup off the cherries, dry them thoroughly and cut them into quarters.

8 oz butter (room temperature) (225 g)
8 oz caster sugar (225 g)
4 eggs, whisked lightly
8 oz plain flour (225 g)
½ teaspoon baking powder
9 oz glacé cherries, prepared as above (250 g)
4 oz ground almonds (110 g)
a few drops almond essence
2 tablespoons demerara sugar
1 tablespoon milk

Pre-heat the oven to gas mark 4 (350 °F) (180 °C)

First line the base and sides of an 8-inch (20 cm) cake tin with greaseproof paper, then cream the butter and sugar together until light, pale and fluffy. Now gradually beat in the whisked egg a little at a time. Then sift the flour and baking powder together, and carefully fold this into the creamed mixture using a metal spoon. Toss the quartered cherries in together, with the ground almonds, and carefully fold these into the cake, adding one or two drops of almond essence and the milk. Now spoon the cake mix into the prepared tin, level off the top with the back of a spoon, then sprinkle with the demerara sugar. Bake the cake in the centre of the oven for one hour, cover with foil and continue cooking for a further 30 minutes, or until the cake has shrunk away from the side of the tin and the centre is springy to touch. Cool the cake in the tin for 15 minutes before turning it out on to a wire rack to cool. Store in a tin.

Rice Cake

This has a good flavour and a nice crumbly texture and is an ideal cake for those who don't like fruit cakes.

4 oz butter (room temperature) (110 g)
8 oz caster sugar (225 g)
the grated rind of 1 lemon
3 eggs
8 oz ground rice (225 g)

Pre-heat the oven to gas mark 4 (350 °F) (180 °C)

First brush a 7-inch (18 cm) round cake tin with melted butter. Line the base and sides with greaseproof paper, then paint the paper with a little melted butter.

Now cream the butter and sugar together with the lemon rind until light, pale and fluffy. Next separate the eggs, placing the whites in a clean, grease-free bowl. Beat the egg yolks first on their own, then into the creamed mixture a little at a time, beating vigorously after each addition. Next whisk the egg whites until they form soft peaks, then fold them carefully into the mixture, together with the ground rice. Now spoon the mixture evenly into the prepared tin and bake on the centre shelf for about 1 hour. Cool in the tin for 10 minutes before turning it out on to a wire tray to cool.

Iced Date and Walnut Cake

This is a very easy mixture to make and the tangy lemon in the icing on the finished cake contrasts beautifully with the spiciness.

8 fl oz boiling water (225 ml)
1 teaspoon bicarbonate of soda
1 oz butter (25 g)
1 egg
5 oz soft dark brown sugar (150 g)
1 teaspoon vanilla essence
6 oz dates, stoned and chopped (175 g)
3 oz ground almonds (75 g)
3 oz chopped walnuts (75 g)
8 oz plain flour, (225 g) sifted with 2 level teaspoons baking
    powder, ¼ teaspoon salt, 1 teaspoon mixed spice, 1 teaspoon
    cinnamon, ½ teaspoon ground cloves, ½ teaspoon ground
    nutmeg

For the icing:
4 oz icing sugar, sifted (110 g)
the grated rind of ½ lemon
½ oz melted butter (10 g)
1 tablespoon lemon juice
1 dessertspoon single cream

Pre-heat the oven to gas mark 4 (350 °F) (180 °C)

One 7- or 8-inch (19–20 cm) cake tin with a loose base, well greased.

In a small bowl pour the boiling water over the dates. Add the bicarbonate of soda, then the butter and stir until the butter has melted. Leave to cool. Meanwhile, beat the egg in a large bowl, add the sugar and beat well again, then add the cooled date mixture and all the other cake ingredients. Stir well to mix everything thoroughly together, then pour the mixture into the tin, and put it in the oven just below the centre shelf. Cook for about 1–1¼ hours, or until the top is nicely browned and the centre feels springy. Let the cake stand for a couple of minutes and then turn it out on to a wire rack to cool. For the icing, mix all the ingredients well together, then stand the cake on an upturned plate and cover the top of the cake with icing and let it spread itself evenly over, and dribble lavishly down the sides. Leave it to set for an hour or so. A few walnut halves arranged round the top would finish it off beautifully.

Greek Orange and Almond Cake

This is a cake adapted from a Greek recipe. I think clotted cream is best to spread on top but, if not, whipped cream or full fat cream cheese would do.

4 oz butter or margarine (110 g)
4 oz caster sugar (110 g)
grated rind of 1 orange
2 eggs, beaten (standard)
6 oz semolina (175 g)
3 oz ground almonds (75 g)
2 teaspoons baking powder
3 tablespoons orange juice

For the syrup:
5 oz granulated sugar (150 g)
4 tablespoons water
3 teaspoons lemon juice
3 tablespoons orange juice
1 inch cinnamon stick (2·5 cm)

For the topping:
¼ pint clotted cream (150 ml)
1 oz blanched, toasted almonds (25 g)

Pre-heat the oven to gas mark 6 (400 °F) (200 °C)

Line a greased 8-inch (20 cm) sandwich tin with a circle of grease-proof paper; grease the paper.

Begin by creaming the butter, sugar and orange rind together in a bowl until light and fluffy then gradually beat in the eggs, a little at a time, beating well between each addition.

Now carefully fold in the semolina, almonds, baking powder and orange juice. Then spoon the cake mixture into the prepared tin and bake it in the centre of the oven for 10 minutes. Then lower the temperature to gas mark 4, (350 °F) (180 °C) and bake for a further 30 minutes or until the cake is golden brown and has shrunk slightly from the side of the tin. Leave it to cool for 5 minutes in the tin then turn it out on to a wire rack and turn it the right way up. To make the syrup, simply combine the sugar and water with the cinnamon stick in a small saucepan. Bring it to a gentle boil and then simmer for about 5 minutes. Then take the pan off the heat. Fish out the cinnamon stick and stir in the orange and lemon juices. Now pour the syrup over the cake. It will look far too much—but don't worry—the cake will eventually absorb it all. Then cover and leave it in a cool place overnight. Just before serving spread the top of the cake with clotted cream—which must be room temperature in order to spread easily—then sprinkle with toasted almonds and serve.

Old-fashioned Seed Cake

This is a very easy family cake, with the good old-fashioned flavour of caraway seeds.

4 oz butter (room temperature) (110 g)
4 oz caster sugar (110 g)
2 large eggs, beaten
5 oz self-raising flour, sifted (150 g)
1 oz ground almonds (25 g)
2–3 tablespoons milk
2 rounded teaspoons caraway seeds
2 tablespoons demerara sugar
1 tablespoon flaked almonds, crushed a bit

Pre-heat the oven to gas mark 4 (350 °F) (180 °C)

A greased 7-inch (18 cm) round cake tin with the base lined with greaseproof paper.

First cream the butter and sugar together until the mixture is pale and fluffy, then gradually beat in the beaten eggs a little at a time. When all the egg has been incorporated, take a metal spoon and lightly fold in the ground almonds, caraway seeds and flour. Then add enough milk to give a good dropping consistency and spoon the mixture into the prepared tin. Level off the surface with the back of a spoon then sprinkle the demerara sugar and crushed almonds all over. Bake in the centre of the oven for about an hour or until the cake shows signs of shrinking away from the sides of the tin. Cool in the tin for 10 minutes, then turn out on to a wire rack to cool. I think that this cake tastes better after a day or two, so wrap it in foil and keep it in a tin.

Honey and Spice Cake

This is another one of those cakes that seems to improve with keeping—so try and make it two or three days in advance if possible.

8 oz plain flour (225 g)
4 oz butter (110 g)
3 oz caster sugar (75 g)
1 level teaspoon ground ginger
1 level teaspoon ground cinnamon
¼ teaspoon ground cloves
finely grated zest of a small orange and a small lemon
1 large egg, beaten
3 oz clear, runny honey (75 g)
1 level teaspoon bicarbonate of soda
2 oz finely chopped mixed candied peel (50 g)

For the icing:
4 oz sifted icing sugar (110 g)
1½ tablespoons lemon juice
2 tablespoons warm water

To decorate:
6 pieces of crystallised ginger, chopped

Pre-heat the oven to gas mark 3 (325 °F) (170 °C)

73

One 7-inch (18 cm) square tin, lightly buttered.

First of all weigh a cup or a small basin on the scales then weigh 3 oz (75 g) of honey into it. Now place the bowl into a saucepan containing barely simmering water and warm the honey a little but be careful it mustn't be too hot, just warm. Next sift the flour and spices into a large mixing bowl then add the sugar and the orange and lemon zest. Now add the butter in small pieces and then rub it lightly into the flour, using your fingertips, until the mixture becomes crumbly. Next, lightly mix in the beaten egg, using a large fork, followed by the warm honey. Then in a small basin mix the bicarbonate of soda with 3 tablespoons of cold water, stir until dissolved, then add to it the cake mixture and beat, quite hard, until the mixture is smooth and soft. Then, finally, stir in the mixed peel and spoon the mixture into the prepared tin, spreading it out evenly. Bake the cake just above the centre of the oven for about 30 minutes or until well risen and springy to touch. Cool it for about 10 minutes, then turn it out on to a wire rack to get quite cold.

Meanwhile prepare the icing by sifting icing sugar into a bowl, then add 2 tablespoons of warm water along with the lemon juice and mix to a thin consistency that will coat the back of a spoon. If you don't think it's thin enough add a spot more water. Now place the cake on a wire rack, with a large place underneath, and pour the icing all over, letting it run down and coat the sides a bit. Then decorate the top with the chopped ginger and store in a tin until needed.

Apricot Crumble Cake

This is a sort of half-flan and half-cake, with a sponge base, fruit filling and crumble topping.

For the cake:
4 oz dried apricots, soaked overnight (110 g)
4 oz self-raising flour (110 g)
pinch of salt

2 oz caster sugar (50 g)
2 oz soft margarine (room temperature) (50 g)
1 standard egg
¼ teaspoon pure almond essence
2 tablespoons milk

For the crumble:
3 oz self-raising flour (75 g)
2 oz caster sugar (50 g)
1 oz butter or margarine (room temperature) (25 g)

For the topping:
1 teaspoon ground cinnamon
1 tablespoon demerara sugar

Pre-heat the oven to gas mark 4 (350 °F) (180 °C)

One 8-inch (20 cm) cake tin, greased and lined.

First prepare the crumble mixture by rubbing the fat into the flour until crumbly. Add the sugar then sprinkle in a dessert-spoon of water and mix with a fork until coarse and lumpy. Then leave the mixture on one side.

Now prepare the cake by placing the remaining flour, salt, margarine, sugar, egg, essence and milk together in a bowl. Beat for a couple of minutes or until the mixture is smooth and evenly blended then spread the mix evenly in the base of the cake tin. Next, drain the apricots in a sieve, then tip them on to some kitchen paper to dry them a bit. Now arrange them lightly—close together—on top of the cake mix. Finally sprinkle the crumble filling over the top and bake in the centre of the oven for about 1 hour. Leave the cake to cool for 20 minutes in the tin before removing it and sprinkling it with the combined cinnamon and brown sugar. Keep this in a tin and you'll find it keeps very well as the apricots stay moist.

Children's Cake

I've called this one 'Children's Cake', because it's made in a large tin and then iced and cut into squares, and it does seem to go a long way in the school holidays etc. Also, you can use different toppings on different sections of the cake, for a party.

8 oz plain flour (225 g)
4 oz sugar (110 g)
4 oz margarine (110 g)
2 teaspoons cream of tartar
1 teaspoon bicarbonate of soda
3 fl oz milk (75 ml)
2 eggs

For the topping:
5 oz icing sugar, sieved (150 g)
juice of a small lemon
some desiccated coconut

Pre-heat the oven to gas mark 3 (325 °F) (170 °C)

For this you will need a square baking tin 10 × 10 inches (25·5 × 25·5 cm) greased and lined with greaseproof paper, also lightly greased.

First, combine the flour, sugar, cream of tartar and bicarbonate of soda in a large mixing bowl. Now gently melt the margarine in a small saucepan. In a smaller bowl, beat the eggs thoroughly. Pour the melted margarine into the beaten eggs, then pour this mixture on to the dry ingredients stirring to blend thoroughly. Lastly, add the milk, then pour the mixture into the prepared tin and bake on the centre shelf for about 35 minutes, or until the centre feels springy.

Let the cake cool in the tin for about 10 minutes, then turn it out on to a wire cooling rack. When absolutely cool pour the icing on, which you make by sifting the icing sugar into a bowl and mixing with the lemon juice. It should have the consistency of thin cream. Spread all over the top of the cake and then sprinkle with desiccated coconut. Serve cut into small squares.

Wholefood Cakes

Once upon a time wholefoods were dismissed as nutty and cranky, and even now those rows and rows of strange pills and potions in healthfood shops do little to dispel this idea. However, there is now some very sound medical opinion from all over the world, to the effect that too much refined food is bad for us. Having gone into it quite thoroughly, I am fairly convinced—like a lot of others who are, more and more, turning to wholewheat bread, for instance.

Of course bread is a staple food; cakes (I should hope) are not, and I can't yet envisage a situation where I would ban white flour or sugar from my kitchen entirely. At the same time I have experimented regularly with wholewheat flour in my cake-making, and been delighted to find that not only is it as good as white flour in some cases, sometimes it's actually better. I was amazed, for example, when I first made an all-in-one sponge cake with wholewheat flour, to discover how good it was: now I actually prefer it in a plain sponge. There are several different types of wholewheat flour on the market—and I can recommend Allinson's as being consistently good as well as widely available.

Wholewheat Guinness Cake

This is a very good 'keeping' cake, as it stays nice and moist and seems to go a long way.

8 oz margarine (room temperature) (225 g)
8 oz light soft brown sugar (225 g)
2 standard eggs, beaten (room temperature)
12 oz wholewheat flour (350 g)
2 teaspoons baking powder
1 teaspoon mixed spice
6 oz currants (175 g)
6 oz sultanas (175 g)
3 oz walnuts, not too finely chopped (75 g)
the grated rind of 1 orange
1 tablespoon orange marmalade
¼ pint Guinness (150 ml)

For the topping:
1 oz flaked almonds, crushed a little bit (25 g)
2 tablespoons demerara sugar

Pre-heat the oven to gas mark 2 (300 °F) (150 °C)

First of all line the base and sides of a 7½- or 8-inch (19 or 20 cm) cake tin (a deep one) with greaseproof paper and brush the paper with some melted margarine.

Now, sieve the brown sugar into a large bowl (sifting removes any hard lumps). Then add the margarine and beat until the mixture becomes fluffy and light. Then gradually beat in the eggs, a little at a time, beating well between each addition. Now combine the flour, baking powder and mixed spice together, then carefully fold in the flour mixture— about 2 heaped tablespoons at a time—alternately with 2 tablespoons of Guinness. When all the stout and dry ingredients have been added, gently fold in the fruit, nuts, grated orange peel and marmalade, then spoon the mixture into the prepared tin. Level the top with the back of a spoon and sprinkle with the demerara sugar and flaked almonds.

Now bake the cake in the centre of the oven for about 2¼–2½ hours or until the cake shows signs of shrinking away from the side of the tin and the centre feels firm and springy. Then remove the cake from the oven and leave it to cool for about 30 minutes before taking it out of the tin. When it's cool, wrap it in greaseproof paper and store in an airtight tin for a few days before eating.

Whole Oat Flapjacks ·(Makes about 10)

Everybody loves flapjacks and I think making them with whole oats (available at wholefood shops)—sometimes called 'Jumbo' oats—adds an extra dimension.

4 oz soft brown sugar (110 g)
4 oz butter or margarine (175 g)
1 rounded dessertspoon golden syrup
6 oz whole oats (or porridge oats) (175 g)
¾ teaspoon ground ginger

Pre-heat the oven to gas mark 2 (300 °F) (150 °C)

A 7- or 8-inch (18 or 20 cm) square baking tin at least 1½ inches (4 cm) deep, lightly greased.

First place the sugar, fat and golden syrup together in a saucepan and heat it gently until the fat has melted, giving it a stir now and then. Take the saucepan off the heat and stir in the porridge oats and ginger, mixing thoroughly. Now pour the mixture into the prepared tin and press it out evenly, using a tablespoon or the back of your hand. Bake in the centre of the oven for 40–45 minutes. Then allow the mixture to cool in the tin for 10 minutes before cutting into oblong bars. Leave in the tin until quite cold before removing them. Store in a tin.

Wheatmeal Madeira Cake

Personally I think a Madeira cake made with half wholewheat flour is far nicer than the usual kind made with all white flour.

8 oz butter or margarine (room temperature) (225 g)
6 oz soft brown sugar, sieved (175 g)
6 oz plain white flour (175 g)
6 oz wholewheat flour (175 g)
3 teaspoons baking powder
pinch of salt
3 standard eggs, beaten
the grated rind of 1 large lemon
5 to 6 tablespoons milk to mix

Pre-heat the oven to gas mark 3 (325 °F) (170 °C)

A 2-lb (900 g) loaf tin greased and the base and sides lined with greaseproof paper.

Start by creaming the fat and sugar together until light and fluffy. Gradually add the beaten eggs, a little at a time, beating well between each addition. Then fold in small batches of the flour, salt and baking powder alternately with tablespoons of milk. When all the flour has been added the mixture should just have a dropping consistency but be a little stiffer than that of a sponge. Lastly fold in the lemon rind. Then spread the mixture into the loaf tin and bake for 1¼–1½ hours, or until the cake has risen and feels springy in the centre. Leave it to cool in the tin for 10 minutes before turning it out on to a wire rack to cool.

If you like, you can lightly place a thin slice of candied citron peel on the surface of the cake before baking or, alternatively, you could finish it off with a layer of lemon icing (i.e. 3 oz sifted icing sugar [75 g] mixed with the juice of half a small lemon).

Chunky Apple Cake

This is another cake which can be served warm as a pudding, topped with whipped cream, or cold as a cake—or both as there's enough for about eight servings.

3 oz butter or margarine (room temperature) (75 g)
6 oz soft brown sugar, sieved (175 g)
4 oz plain white flour (110 g)
4 oz wholewheat flour (110 g)
½ teaspoon mixed spice
½ teaspoon ground cinnamon
2 large eggs, beaten
a little milk
2 teaspoons baking powder
1 tablespoon chopped mixed peel
grated rind of 1 orange
3 cooking apples (about 1¼ lb/550 g)

Pre-heat the oven to gas mark 4 (350 °F) (180 °C)

A greased 8½-inch (21·5 cm) cake tin, lined and the lining paper brushed with melted fat.

First sift the flours, spices and baking powder on to a sheet of greaseproof paper. If you're left with some bran in the sieve at the end, tip that in too. Now peel, core and dice the apples into small cubes, then transfer them to a bowl and toss with a heaped tablespoon of the sieved flour mixture.

Then in a separate bowl beat the fat and sugar together until fluffy and pale beige. After that gradually beat in the eggs, a little at a time. Then carefully fold in the flour mixture and, lastly, the grated orange rind, mixed peel and diced apple. If the mixture seems a little dry, add a spot of milk. Now spoon the cake mix into the prepared tin and level it off with the back of a spoon. Then bake in the centre of the oven for about one hour or until the cake feels springy in the centre when lightly pressed with a fingertip and just shows signs of shrinking away from the edge of the tin. Cool in the tin for 10 minutes before turning out and this looks nice dusted with sifted icing sugar just before serving.

Fruit Bran Loaf

This really is one of the easiest cakes in the book—and one of my own favourites. All you have to do is to remember to assemble some of the ingredients the night before and next day it's made in moments.

4 oz All Bran breakfast cereal (110 g)
2 oz soft brown sugar (50 g)
10 oz mixed dried fruit (275 g)
⅓ teaspoon mixed spice
½ pint milk (275 ml)
4 oz wholewheat self-raising flour (110 g)

The night before cooking this, measure the All Bran, sugar and fruit into a mixing bowl, mix it thoroughly then stir in the milk. Cover with a cloth and leave overnight to soak.

Next day pre-heat the oven to gas mark 4 (350 °F) (180 °C)

Add the wholemeal self-raising flour and spice into the soaked mixture. Stir and mix well, then spoon the mixture into a very well greased 2-lb (900 g) loaf tin, and bake for about 1 hour. Then loosen with a palette knife, turn the loaf out on to a wire tray to cool, and serve if you like spread with butter—but I think it's nice on its own.

Note: White self-raising flour can be used instead of wholewheat if you prefer.

Wholewheat Coffee Cake

4 oz plain wholewheat flour (Allinsons) (110 g)
2½ level teaspoons baking powder
4 oz soft tub margarine (110 g)
4 oz soft brown sugar (110 g)
2 large eggs
2 heaped teaspoons instant coffee
1 dessertspoon hot water
milk

Then for the filling and topping:
¼ pint (150 ml) double cream whipped with a level tablespoon
of caster sugar
2 teaspoons instant coffee, mixed with 1 dessertspoon hot
water
2 oz (50 g) chopped walnuts

Pre-heat the oven to gas mark 3 (325 °F) (170 °C)

First line the bases of two well-greased 7-inch (18 cm) sandwich tins (at least 1 inch [2·5 cm] deep) with circles of greaseproof paper and lightly grease that too.

Then combine the first amount of instant coffee with the hot
water, then place it along with all the cake ingredients in a large
bowl and whisk, till the mix is thoroughly blended (about one
minute). Then you should have a good 'dropping' consistency.
If not, add about 1 dessertspoon of milk. Now divide the
mixture and spread it evenly in the two tins, and bake on the
centre shelf of the oven for about 30 minutes or until springy.
After 30 seconds, loosen the sponges with a palette knife all
round then turn them out on to a cooling tray. When they're
cool combine the topping and filling ingredients together, using
half the walnuts. Then sandwich the sponges together with
half the filling and spread the rest over the top, sprinkled with
the rest of the walnuts. Store, covered, in the lowest part of the
refrigerator—that's if there's any left!

Whole Oat Slices

If you've never made a cake in your life you'll be able to tackle these very easy, very delicious oat slices. They taste best made with Jumbo oats, available at wholefood shops but, if you can't get hold of them, ordinary porridge oats will do.

3 oz whole Jumbo oats (75 g)
3 oz wholewheat flour (75 g)
1½ oz brown sugar (40 g)
3 oz butter or margarine (75 g)
¾ teaspoon baking powder

For the filling:
8 oz (225 g) dates (simmered in water for about 10 minutes until soft), or 6 oz (175 g) pre-soaked dried apricots, chopped or 8 oz (225 g) mincemeat

Pre-heat the oven to gas mark 4 (350 °F) (180 °C)

A well-greased oblong tin 11 × 7 inches (28 × 18 cm).

First measure the dry ingredients into a bowl, then rub in the fat quite thoroughly. Next sprinkle half the mixture over the base of the tin and, using your hands, press and even it out to form a base without any gaps. Then arrange the filling carefully all over this. Then sprinkle the rest of the mixture evenly over the filling and press this down firmly all over. Bake for about 30–40 minutes. Leave in the tin for 10 minutes, then cut into squares, cool on a wire rack and store in an airtight tin.

Wholewheat Gingerbread

This is my favourite Gingerbread. It's very dark, very moist and keeps beautifully.

4 oz margarine (110 g)
6 oz black treacle (175 g) ⎱ Weigh a small saucepan first, then
⎰ add the 6 oz (175 g) black treacle
2 oz golden syrup (50 g) ⎰ followed by the syrup.
¼ pint milk (150 ml)
2 standard eggs
1 teaspoon bicarbonate of soda
4 oz plain flour (110 g)
4 oz wholewheat flour (110 g)
2 oz soft light brown sugar (50 g)
2 teaspoons mixed spice
3 teaspoons ground ginger
2 oz crystallised ginger (50 g)
2 oz sultanas (50 g)

For the topping:
Additional black treacle and 4 tablespoons chopped crystallised
    ginger

Pre-heat the oven to gas mark 2 (300 °F) (150 °C)

Brush a 7-inch (18 cm) square cake tin with melted fat. Line the tin's base with greaseproof paper; brush the paper with melted fat.

Begin by placing the margarine in the saucepan with the treacle and syrup and then heat them together, gently, until the margarine has melted. Then take the pan from the heat and stir in the milk. Now beat the eggs and add those to the mixture too.

Combine the dry ingredients in a bowl (sieving the sugar if it seems lumpy). Then stir the syrup liquid into the flour etc and when it's smoothly blended add the sultanas and chopped crystallised ginger. Pour the mixture into the prepared tin and bake in the centre of the oven for 1¼–1½ hours, or until the gingerbread begins to shrink away slightly from the side of the tin and the centre is springy to touch.

Now remove the Gingerbread from the oven and leave to cool in the tin for 10 minutes. Brush the top quite liberally with some more black treacle (warmed a little first to make it spread more easily) and press a few pieces of chopped ginger on to the surface; then leave it to cool. Remove from the tin and store in an airtight tin, cutting it across in slices to serve.

Wholewheat Chocolate Fudge Cake

This is another wholewheat sponge made by the all-in-one method, and it has a delicious chocolate fudge filling and topping.

4 oz plain wholewheat flour (100 g)
2½ level teaspoons baking powder
4 oz soft margarine (110 g)
4 oz soft brown sugar (110 g)
2 large eggs
1 slightly rounded tablespoon cocoa powder (unsweetened)

For the chocolate fudge :
3 oz soft brown sugar (75 g)
1½ oz butter (40 g)
3 oz unsweetened baker's chocolate (or plain chocolate) (75 g)
4 fluid oz evaporated milk (100 ml)
2 drops vanilla essence

Pre-heat the oven to gas mark 3 (325 °F) (170 °C)

For this you will need 2 × 7-inch (18 cm), sandwich tins, at least 1½ inches (4 cm) deep, greased and bases lined with greaseproof paper.

First of all, weigh the flour, then take out 1 rounded table-spoon of flour and replace it with one rounded tablespoon of cocoa. The tablespoon of flour you take out won't be needed. Now simply place all the cake ingredients in a large mixing bowl and beat them together to a good dropping consistency. If the mixture seems a little dry add a little drop of water.

Now divide the mixture and spread it evenly in the prepared

tins and bake on the centre shelf of the oven for about 30 minutes or until springy in the centres. After 30 seconds (or thereabouts) turn the cakes out on to a wire cooling rack and strip off the base papers. Leave to cool while you make chocolate fudge.

To do this, combine the sugar and evaporated milk in a heavy saucepan. Heat gently to dissolve the sugar, stirring frequently. When the sugar is dissolved and the mixture comes to the boil, keep the heat very low and simmer for 6 minutes without stirring. Remove the pan from the heat, add the chocolate, broken up, stir to dissolve the chocolate then stir in the butter and vanilla essence. When the mixture is cool cover it with foil or clingfilm and chill until mixture thickens.

Then beat again, and spread half on one sponge, placing the other one on top. Use the rest to spread over the top and, if you like, decorate with walnut halves or flaked, toasted almonds.

Chocolatey Cakes

I'm afraid I have a terrible weakness for anything chocolatey: although I rarely buy boxes or bars, chocolate puddings and cakes are totally irresistible. So I fear I have indulged myself completely in this chapter and allowed my chocolate-coated imagination to run riot. I'm sorry if you have to diet. I do too, most of the time, but every now and then we all need cheering up with something gooey and squidgy and very chocolatey.

One thing though. As a hardened chocolate addict I really feel that too much sugar often spoils chocolate cakes. So to get the real flavour of chocolate, rather than just an impression of concentrated sweetness, I think sugar in recipes should be kept to a minimum: the best sort of chocolate cake should be dark and sophisticated! For the most part commercially made plain chocolate is often very sweet, so never use sugar with it.

In some cakes I've recommended proper, unsweetened baker's chocolate which is not as widely available as one would like, but delicatessens and wholefood shops usually stock it and it's worth buying a good supply when you see it. Failing baker's chocolate, bitter dessert chocolate would be my second choice—the so-called cooking chocolate available in supermarkets is, I find, a little synthetic (as the list of weird ingredients on the packet confirms). Where cocoa powder is called for, by the way, I do mean proper cocoa powder and not drinking chocolate.

Black Forest Cake   (Serves 6–8)

This is my adaptation of the German Black Forest gâteau. It's very dark, moist and chocolatey as there's no flour in it and then it's sandwiched together with cream and bitter cherries.

6 large eggs
5 oz caster sugar (150 g)
2 oz cocoa powder—sieved (50 g)
½ pint double cream (275 ml)
1 level tablespoon caster sugar
1 × 1-lb tin or jar of morello cherries (450 g)
2 oz plain chocolate (50 g)
3 tablespoons kirsch (or rum)

Pre-heat the oven to gas mark 4 (350 °F) (180 °C)

2 × 8-inch (20 cm) sandwich tins, oiled with a tasteless groundnut oil and the bases lined with greaseproof paper also oiled.

Start off by separating the eggs and placing the whites in a clean grease-free bowl. Put the yolks in another bowl and whisk them with the caster sugar until they just begin to pale and thicken (be careful not to thicken them too much though). Now fold in the sieved cocoa powder.

Then with a clean whisk, beat the egg whites until stiff but not too dry. Stir a heaped tablespoon of the egg white into the chocolate mixture to loosen it up a little bit. Then, using a metal spoon, carefully and gently fold in the rest of the egg white. Try not to lose any air. Divide the mixture equally into the prepared sandwich tins and bake them near the centre of the oven for about 15–20 minutes. They won't appear to be cooked exactly, just set and slightly puffy and, when you take them out of the oven, they'll shrink quite a lot but that's normal so don't worry. Leave the cakes to cool in the tins but turn them out while they're still faintly warm and strip off the base papers.

Now whip the cream with the tablespoon of caster sugar until it's a 'floppy' spreadable consistency.

Next empty the tin of cherries into a sieve over a bowl and combine 2 tablespoons of the juice with 1 tablespoon of kirsch. Sprinkle this over the cake layers and, using a palette knife, spread about a third of the whipped cream over one cake. Then slice the cherries and de-pip them—if they have pips, some brands don't. Leave about a dozen whole ones though for the decoration. Now arrange the sliced cherries all over the cake spread with cream. Next, carefully place the other cake on top and cover the entire cake with the remaining cream, again using a palette knife. Finish off by arranging the whole cherries around the edge, then grate the chocolate and sprinkle it all over.

Note: If you can't get morello cherries, any tinned black cherries would do and, if you prefer not to cover the entire cake with cream, you could spread half of it in the middle and half on top.

Brownies

These moist, chewy, chocolate nut squares beloved by native Americans make compulsive eating, I find, so I *try* not to make them too often!

2 oz unsweetened baker's chocolate (if possible, if not use
    plain chocolate) (50 g)
4 oz butter (110 g)
2 eggs beaten
8 oz granulated sugar (225 g)
2 oz plain flour (50 g)
1 teaspoon baking powder
¼ teaspoon salt
4 oz chopped nuts (110 g) (these can be walnuts, almonds,
    hazelnuts, or best of all Brazils)

Pre-heat the oven to gas mark 4 (350 °F) (180 °C)

First line the base of a well-greased oblong tin measuring 7 × 11 inches (18 × 28 cm) with greaseproof paper.

Then melt the butter and broken up chocolate together in the top of a double saucepan (or else place it in a basin fitted over simmering water on a very low heat). Then simply stir in all the remaining ingredients, spread the mixture in the lined tin and bake for 30 minutes, or until a knife inserted in the centre of the mixture comes out cleanly. Then leave the mixture in the tin to cool for 10 minutes before dividing into, roughly, fifteen squares and transferring them to a wire rack to finish cooling.

Gâteau Belle Hélène (Serves 6–8)

This makes a delicious party pud in the autumn when William pears are available.

2 oz unsweetened (preferably) chocolate or plain chocolate (50 g)
4 tablespoons water
3 eggs
4½ oz caster sugar (125 g)
2½ oz plain flour (60 g)

Then for the filling:
½ pint double cream (275 ml)
2 *ripe* pears
1 tablespoon caster sugar
a little rum if you have some
a little grated chocolate

Pre-heat the oven to gas mark 4 (350 °F) (180 °C)

First liberally butter a 7-inch (18 cm) cake tin with a removable base. Line the base with greaseproof paper and butter that too.

Now melt the chocolate in the water in a basin set over a saucepan of barely simmering water. While that's happening place the eggs and sugar together in a bowl and whisk until pale and fluffy. Then pour in the melted chocolate and carefully fold it into the mixture, followed by the sieved flour. Pour the mixture into the prepared cake tin and bake in the centre of the oven for about 40–45 minutes, or until the cake shows signs of shrinking away from the sides of the tin. Turn the cake out on to a wire rack and leave it to cool. Next whisk the sugar and cream together with a tablespoon of rum until thickened. Then peel, quarter, core and thinly slice the pears. Cut the cake into two rounds, sprinkle the cut surfaces with a little rum and spread both surfaces with half the whipped cream. Arrange the sliced pears on the base half of the cake, and cover with the top half. Now use the remaining cream to spread all over the cake. Sprinkle with grated chocolate and chill lightly until ready to serve.

Chocolate Soured Cream Cake

The filling and topping on this cake has a really dark chocolatey flavour which I like very much; if, however, you'd like it sweeter add 1 tablespoon of caster sugar to the chocolate when you melt it.

4 oz self-raising flour, sifted (110 g)
1 level teaspoon baking powder
4 oz caster sugar (110 g)
2 large fresh eggs
4 oz soft margarine (110 g)
2 tablespoons sieved cocoa powder (not drinking chocolate)
1 tablespoon milk

For the topping:
5 oz semi-sweet plain chocolate (150 g)
1 × 5 oz carton soured cream (150 ml)
a few walnut halves or toasted chopped hazelnuts to decorate

Pre-heat the oven to gas mark 3 (325 °F) (170 °C)

For this you'll need two 7-inch (18 cm) sandwich tins at least 1 inch (2·5 cm) in depth, greased, and the bases lined with greaseproof paper also greased.

For the cake, just put everything in the bowl together and beat thoroughly (or use an electric hand whisk for about one

94

minute) till smooth. Then spoon the mixture into the two prepared sandwich tins, dividing it evenly, and bake them side by side in the centre of the oven for 25–30 minutes. Then turn them straight out on to a wire rack to cool about half a minute after they come out of the oven.

Meanwhile make the topping by breaking the chocolate into a basin fitted over a saucepan of barely simmering water, add the soured cream too, and stir, keeping the heat very low, till the chocolate has melted and you have a smooth cream mixture. Then remove the bowl from the heat and, as soon as it's cool, spread half the mixture over one half of the cake, sandwich them together and spread the rest over the top. Decorate with nuts and store in an airtight tin. I think this one is nicest eaten as fresh as possible.

Chocolate Beer Cake

Sweet stout is used for this cake, which always appeals to men.

4 oz butter or margarine (110 g)
10 oz dark, soft brown sugar (275 g)
2 standard eggs, beaten
6 oz plain flour (175 g)
¼ teaspoon baking powder
1 teaspoon bicarbonate of soda
7 fl oz sweet stout (200 ml)
2 oz cocoa (50 g)

For the icing:
4 oz plain chocolate (110 g)
2 tablespoons sweet stout
2 oz butter (50 g)
4 oz icing sugar, sifted (110 g)
1 oz walnut pieces, finely chopped (25 g)

To decorate:
8 walnut halves
grated chocolate

Pre-heat the oven to gas mark 4 (350 °F) (180 °C)

First brush two 8-inch (20 cm) sandwich tins with melted fat and line the bases with circles of greaseproof paper, also brushed with melted fat.

Then cream the butter and sugar together, beating thoroughly for about 3 or 4 minutes until pale and fluffy. Now gradually beat in the eggs, a little at a time, beating well between each addition. Next sift the flour, baking powder and bicarbonate of soda on to a sheet of greaseproof paper. Then weigh the cocoa and put in a separate bowl—gradually stirring the stout into it. Now carefully and lightly fold into the mixture small quantities of the sifted flour alternately with the cocoa–stout liquid. Then when both have been added, divide the cake mixture equally between the two tins and level it out. Bake the sponges in the centre of the oven for 30–35 minutes. The cakes should be flat on top and feel springy and will have shrunk slightly from the side of the tin. Leave them to cool in the tins for 5 minutes before turning out on to a wire rack to cool further. To make the icing melt the chocolate with the stout in a bowl set over a pan of hot water. Then when it's melted remove the bowl from the water and beat in the butter and leave it to cool a little before beating in the icing sugar. Now remove a quarter of the icing to a separate bowl and stir in the chopped walnuts. After the icings have cooled to a spreadable consistency, sandwich the cake with the walnut icing. Then spread the top and sides of the cake with the rest, smoothing it over with a palette knife. Now arrange the walnut halves at regular intervals around the top edge of the cake and sprinkle lightly with the grated chocolate. Now try to be patient and allow the icing to become firm before eating!

Chocolate Log with Chestnut Filling

This is my version of the famous *Bûche de Noël*, which is eaten at Christmas time all over France. It's very rich but light and absolutely scrumptious!

5 oz caster sugar (150 g)
6 large eggs, separated
2 oz cocoa powder (50 g)
1 × 8¾ oz tin sweetened chestnut purée (*crème de marron*) (240 g)
½ pint double cream (275 ml)
icing sugar

Pre-heat the oven to gas mark 4 (350 °F) (180 °C)

You'll also need a tin 11½ × 7 inches (29 × 18 cm) and about 1 inch (2·5 cm) deep, oiled and lined with greaseproof paper (also lightly oiled).

First place the egg yolks in a basin and whisk until they start to thicken, then add the caster sugar and continue to whisk until the mixture starts to thicken slightly—but be careful not to get it *too* thick. Now mix the cocoa powder into the egg yolk mixture then, using a clean whisk and bowl, beat up the egg whites to the soft peak stage. Next carefully cut and fold the egg white into the chocolate mixture—gently and thoroughly—then pour the mixture into the prepared tin. Bake on the centre shelf for 20–25 minutes until springy and puffy—then remove it from the oven (it will shrink quite a bit but don't worry, that's normal). Cool it, then arrange an oblong of greaseproof paper on a work-surface and dust it liberally all over with icing sugar. Invert the cake tin over it to remove the sponge. Now peel off the greaseproof paper and carefully spread the chestnut purée all over followed by the whipped cream, and then gently roll it up to a log shape. The icing sugar will look like snow and if the log cracks slightly this can look quite attractive; and at Christmas a sprig of holly on top looks very seasonal.

Moist Chocolate and Rum Squares

These are rich and chocolatey and very fattening I should think!

5 oz butter or margarine (150 g)
5 oz caster sugar (150 g)
5 oz plain chocolate, grated (150 g)
5 oz ground almonds (150 g)
5 eggs, separated (standard)

For the icing:
4 oz plain chocolate (110 g)
2 tablespoons rum
1 tablespoon cream
2 oz blanched, toasted almonds, chopped (50 g)

Pre-heat the oven to gas mark 3 (325 °F) (170 °C)

Brush a tin 11 × 7 × 1¼ inches (28 × 18 × 3 cm) with melted fat, then line the base with greaseproof paper and brush that also with melted fat.

First cream the butter and sugar until pale, light and fluffy. Beat in the egg yolks bit by bit. Then carefully fold in the almonds and grated chocolate. Now, whisk the egg whites to a soft foam—not too stiff—and fold them into the chocolate mixture. Spread the mixture into the prepared tin and bake in the centre of the oven for about 55 minutes to 1 hour. Leave the cake to cool in the tin then loosen the edges and turn it out on to a wire rack and strip off the lining paper turning it the right way up afterwards. Now put the chocolate in a bowl over a pan of hot water. When it's melted, take it off the heat and stir in the cream and 1 tablespoon rum, then let the icing cool and thicken a bit. Sprinkle the surface of the cake with the other tablespoon of rum, and spread with the cooled chocolate icing. Scatter the toasted almonds all over and leave until cold and set before cutting into squares.

Moist Chocolate and Almond Cake

This is a beautifully moist cake, light in colour, but with dark speckles of melted chocolate in it.

4 oz butter (room temperature) (110 g)
4 oz unsweetened (or plain) chocolate, grated (110 g)
6 oz caster sugar (175 g)
6 tablespoons milk
4 large egg yolks
4 large egg whites
4 oz ground almonds (110 g)
6 oz self-raising flour, sifted (175 g)

To decorate:
6 oz plain chocolate (175 g)
a few toasted flaked almonds

Pre-heat the oven to gas mark 7 (425 °F) (220 °C)

You'll need an 8-inch (20 cm) cake tin, greased and lined.

Start by creaming the butter and sugar together until they're light, pale and fluffy. Beat the egg yolks thoroughly together and add them to the mixture about a teaspoonful at a time, beating well after each addition. When all the yolks are in, lightly fold in the ground almonds, grated chocolate and milk, using a metal spoon. Now in a separate dry, clean, bowl whisk the egg whites till they reach the soft-peak stage, and then fold them into the rest of the mixture gently and carefully so as not to lose all the air you have whisked in. Finally add the flour—again folding that in carefully with a metal spoon. Next spoon the mixture into the prepared tin, level it off, place it on the centre shelf in the oven, reduce the heat to gas mark 3 (325 °F) (170 °C) and bake the cake for 1–1¼ hours or until the centre is springy when lightly touched. Allow the cake to stand in the tin for 5 minutes, then turn it out on to a wire rack to cool. To decorate, melt 6 oz (175 g) of plain chocolate. Allow it to cool and thicken slightly, then split the cake in half. Use half the chocolate to sandwich it together, and the other half to spread over the top, making patterns with a knife. Decorate with a few toasted almonds and store in a tin till needed.

Squidgy Chocolate Cake

This is a soft and squashy chocolate cake serving 8 people. Perhaps better described as half-cake and half-pudding, and never been known not to please.

8 oz dark plain chocolate (225 g)
4 oz caster sugar (110 g)
8 large eggs
2 oz Bourneville cocoa powder (50 g)
¾ pint double cream (425 ml)
2 tablespoons water
Grated chocolate for decoration

Pre-heat the oven to gas mark 4 (350 °F) (180 °C)

You'll need an oblong baking tin, approximately 11½ × 7 inches (29 × 18 cm) and just over 1 inch (2·5 cm) deep, and grease-proof paper.

For the chocolate filling: Break the plain chocolate in pieces into a basin with the water. Place the basin over a saucepan of barely simmering water and wait for the chocolate to melt. Then remove it from the heat and beat with a wooden spoon until smooth. Separate two large eggs and beat the yolks, first on their own, then into the warm chocolate mixture. Let it cool a bit then whisk the egg-whites till stiff and fold them into the chocolate mixture. Cover the bowl and chill in the refrigerator for about an hour.

To make the cake: Oil the cake tin lightly and line it with a suitably sized piece of greaseproof paper (pleating it at the corners so that it fits) and oil the greaseproof paper lightly too. Now separate six large eggs, putting the whites into a large mixing bowl and the yolks into a pudding basin. Whisk the yolks (with a hand whisk or an electric mixer) until they start to thicken, then add the caster sugar and continue to whisk until the mixture feels thick—but don't overdo it, it shouldn't be starting to turn pale. Now, still whisking, add the cocoa powder. Next, using a clean dry whisk, beat the egg whites till they are stiff and form little peaks. At this point, take a metal spoon and carefully fold them into the egg yolk mixture, gently and thoroughly and making sure you get right down to the bottom of the bowl with the spoon. Pour the complete mixture into the prepared tin, spread it evenly and bake on a highish shelf in the oven for about 20–25 minutes. By that time the cake will appear to have risen and will look puffy like a soufflé (it won't look as if it's cooked—but it will be). Remove it from the oven and don't be alarmed as it starts to sink because it's supposed to—when it is cool, it will look crinkly on the surface. To turn it out, place a piece of greaseproof paper on the table, loosen the edges of the cake all round with a knife, then turn the tin upside down on to the paper. Give a few sharp taps, lift the tin away from the cake and carefully peel off the greaseproof paper. Now cut the cake evenly in half down the centre so you have two squares. Take the chocolate filling from the fridge, and whip up the cream until quite thick. Then, using a palette knife, spread half the chocolate mixture carefully over one half of the cake, and about a quarter of the cream over the chocolate. Place the other half of the cake on top, forming a sandwich (a frying-pan slice will assist this rather delicate operation). Spread the rest of the chocolate mixture on top, and cover the whole cake (sides as well) with whipped cream. Decorate the top with grated chocolate, and transfer to a serving dish. If it doesn't all disappear (highly unlikely), keep it covered in the lowest part of the refrigerator.

Sachertorte

I don't pretend that this is from the original recipe from the hotel Sacher, in Vienna, where it is supposed to be a closely guarded secret. However, it is a very good interpretation.

4 oz butter (at room temperature) (110 g)
4 oz caster sugar (110 g)
4 egg yolks, well beaten
6 oz plain chocolate (unsweetened baker's chocolate is best) (175 g)
¼ teaspoon almond essence
4 oz plain flour (110 g)
½ level teaspoon baking powder
5 large egg whites

For the icing:
2 teaspoons apricot jam
4 oz plain chocolate (110 g)
4 tablespoons water
2 teaspoons glycerine
3 oz icing sugar, sifted (75 g)

Pre-heat the oven to gas mark 2 (300 °F) (150 °C)

For this you will need a 7½-inch (19 cm) cake tin, lightly greased and the base lined with greaseproof paper also greased with butter.

Start off by melting the chocolate, break it up into a basin, then place the basin over a saucepan of barely simmering water and leave it to melt slowly, being careful not to let it overheat.

While that's happening, cream the butter and sugar until very pale and fluffy. Now beat in the egg yolks, a little at a time, beating well after each addition. Then, as soon as the chocolate has melted, beat it gradually into the creamed butter mixture and then add the almond essence. Next, sift the flour and baking powder then put it all back into the sieve and sift it into the mixture, a little at a time, carefully folding it in with a metal spoon. When all the flour is incorporated whisk the egg whites until stiff and then carefully fold them into the mixture, bit by bit, still using a metal spoon. Now pour the mixture into the prepared cake tin, level the top and bake it on the middle shelf of the oven for about 1 hour, or until firm and well risen.

When it's cooked, allow the cake to cool in the tin for 10 minutes before turning it out on to a cooling rack. Then leave it to get quite cold.

To make the icing, melt the chocolate with the water, again in a basin over hot water. Then beat in the glycerine and stir in enough sifted icing sugar to give a coating consistency. Now, warm the apricot jam and brush the cake all over with it. Pour the icing over the whole cake using a palette knife to cover the top and sides completely. Then leave it to set. In Vienna, slices of Sachertorte are always served with a dollop of thick whipped cream—but I leave that up to you!

Cakes for Occasions

There are certain recipes that always leave room for improvement: an extra touch of this or that and they can develop. But I can honestly say that so far as my Rich Fruit Cake recipe is concerned, I wouldn't ever change anything. It's more or less my mother's recipe that we have always had at Christmas, birthdays and celebrations—including my own wedding. (It is, I should add, a very rich fruit cake and for those who like one less rich for celebrations I have included a light fruit cake too.)

I find an 8-inch (20 cm) cake just the right size for Christmas, birthdays, christening parties or any function up to 45 people. Weddings will probably call for a combination of the different sizes given. I have added directions for the simple decoration of a cake, that should cover most occasions including Silver or Golden weddings, but should you want to go deeper into the complicated art of icing I can recommend a book called *Cake Decorating and Sugarcraft* by Evelyn Wallace (Newnes Publications), probably available at most public libraries.

NOTES ON RICH FRUIT CAKES

1 *Maturing*

All rich fruit cakes are best made at least eight weeks in advance.
If for some reason you can't manage this, it's not disastrous:
they just *taste* better if they mature.

2 *Fruit*

If you can manage to pre-soak the fruit overnight before you
make the cake, so much the better. Pre-soaking with brandy
will plumpen the fruit and give it extra flavour. If you haven't
got—or don't want to use brandy—orange juice can be used
instead.

3 *Candied Peel*

Ready-cut candied peel never has as good a flavour as whole
candied peel which you chop yourself. Wholefood shops and
delicatessens sell this and as it keeps very well in a tin or jar,
it's worth buying in a regular stock of orange, lemon and citron
peel (the latter is green, and made from the peel of an otherwise
inedible, very bitter, citrus fruit that grows in Mediterranean
countries).

4 *Baking*

Slow baking is best for rich cakes, and to give extra protection
to the edges of the cake line the tins (*see* page 24) with a double
thickness of greaseproof paper inside, then also tie a double
band of thick brown paper around the outside of the tin. To
protect the top of the cake, place a double square of greaseproof on top as well, making a small hole the size of a 50p piece
in the centre.

5 Storing

I like to 'feed' rich fruit cakes with brandy at odd intervals, so I always strip off the lining papers, make a few holes in the top (using a thin darning needle) and pour teaspoonfuls of brandy in to soak down into the cake. Then a week or two later, make small holes in the base and pour a little more brandy and so on.

Always wrap the cake well in a large square of double greaseproof paper: bring the paper up either side, make a pleat to join it, then roll the pleat over and over downwards, and finally fold the two open ends over at each corner bringing them up over the top and securing the whole thing with a thick rubber band. Then store it in a tin—if you don't have a suitably sized tin, you can use double foil *over* the greaseproof, but never wrap the cake directly in foil as the acid in the fruit can cause corrosion, and a mould can develop!

6 Icing

If you intend to ice a cake for a special occasion, it should be almond iced at least seven days before the royal icing is put on —this is so it has a chance to dry out. Otherwise the oil from the almonds can seep through and discolour the icing, making it look rather dirty. Also it is best not to ice a cake too far in advance: about five days before the event is perfect. Of course if, like me, you sometimes find you haven't got around to either before Christmas Eve (for instance), then a thick coating of rough 'snow scene' royal icing slapped straight on top of the almond paste will—happily—be all right.

7 Keeping

How long will a fruit cake keep? This is a question that's always coming up, and I find it difficult to answer. I *have* kept un-iced rich fruit cakes for several months with no adverse effects, but I do feel that iced cakes get a slightly stale taste if they're stored too long. I always feel wary of people who boast of cakes keeping from one year to the next: the short answer is that very often they taste like it!

Traditional Christmas Cake

1 lb currants (450 g)
6 oz sultanas (175 g)
6 oz raisins (175 g)
2 oz glacé cherries, rinsed and finely chopped (50 g)
2 oz mixed peel, finely chopped (50 g)

You should get these first five ingredients ready the night before you make the cake: put them all in a bowl and mix them with 3 tablespoons of brandy, cover with a cloth and leave them to soak for a minimum of 12 hours.

½ lb plain flour (225 g)
¼ teaspoon salt
¼ teaspoon grated nutmeg
½ teaspoon mixed spice
2 oz almonds, blanched, peeled and chopped (50 g)
½ lb soft brown sugar (225 g)
1 dessertspoon black treacle
½ lb unsalted butter (225 g)
4 standard eggs
the grated rind of 1 lemon
the grated rind of 1 orange

Pre-heat the oven to gas mark 1 (275 °F) (145 °C)

An 8-inch (20 cm) round cake tin, or a 7-inch (18 cm) square one, greased and lined with greaseproof paper.

Before you start put the treacle in a warm place (the warming-drawer of the oven) so that it melts a little.

Now sieve the flour, salt and spices into a large mixing bowl, and in another bowl cream the butter and sugar until the mixture is fluffy and light—don't skimp on this, it's the most important part of the cake. When the mixture is creamed, beat the eggs and gradually add them to it—a tablespoonful at a time, and beat thoroughly after each addition (if it looks as if it might start curdling, you can add a little of the flour to help prevent it).

After the egg has been added, fold in the flour and spices—not beating this time, just fold bit by bit. Next stir in the fruit which has been soaking, the nuts and the treacle, and last of all the grated orange and lemon rinds. Spoon the mixture into your prepared cake tin, spreading it out evenly with the back of a dessertspoon, and make a very gentle depression in the centre. (At this stage—if you are not planning to ice the cake, you can arrange a few whole blanched almonds over the top, but *lightly* or they'll disappear into the cake.)

Tie a band of brown paper around the tin, and cover the top of the cake with a square of double greaseproof paper with a hole in the middle approximately the size of a 50p piece. Put the cake on the lower shelf of the oven and leave it to bake—without opening the door—for $4\frac{1}{2}$–$4\frac{3}{4}$ hours. To test if it is cooked, insert a skewer into the centre. If it comes out clean, and you can hear no sizzling noise, the cake is cooked. Store it in an airtight tin and 'feed' it at odd intervals with brandy, as in the notes (p. 108).

CHRISTMAS CAKE ICING

As I've mentioned Christmas can sometimes get the better of me, and it's been not unknown for me to be icing the cake somewhere between Midnight Mass and breakfast. Then all it gets is a rough snow scene and a couple of robins. The trouble is robins are not what they used to be—I don't think the plastic factories in Hong Kong have got to grips with the English Christmas scene at all. So for a really organised Christmas, here is a semi-rough icing in which I've escaped any piping by substituting marzipan poinsettias and a red ribbon to make it look the part.

Almond Paste (to model)

This one is made in a slightly different way from normal almond paste, to make it easier to handle for shaping the decoration.

1 lb ground almonds (450 g)
8 oz caster sugar (225 g)
8 oz icing sugar (225 g)
2 standard eggs
2 egg yolks (the whites should be kept covered in a bowl, and
   reserved for the Royal Icing)
½ teaspoon pure almond essence
1 teaspoon brandy
1 teaspoon lemon juice
Red, green and yellow colouring
Red satin ribbon (1½ inches [4 cm] wide)

Begin by sieving the sugars into a large bowl and stirring in the
eggs and egg yolks. Put the bowl over a pan of barely simmering
water and whisk for about 12 minutes until the mixture is thick
and fluffy. Then remove the bowl from the heat and sit the base
in a couple of inches of cold water. Next whisk in the essence,
brandy and lemon juice and carry on whisking until the mixture's cool. Finally stir in the ground almonds and knead to
form a firm paste. Weigh and separate 6 oz (175 g) of paste
(for the decoration) and put on one side in a bowl covered with
clingfilm.

Divide the rest of the paste in half, and roll out one piece to
a circle approx 1 inch (2·5 cm) larger than the top of the cake
(your work-surface should be kept dusted with some sifted icing
sugar). Brush the top of the cake with egg white, then invert
the cake to sit centrally on the almond paste, and with a palette
knife press the paste up around the edge of the cake. Turn it
the right way up now, then brush the side with egg white.

Roll out the other half of paste to a rectangle and trim it so it
measures half the circumference of the cake by twice the height
of the cake—a piece of string will help you to measure these
lengths accurately. Now cut the paste rectangle in half lengthways, and lightly press the two strips on to the side of the cake.
Smooth over the joints with a knife, and leave the cake covered
with a cloth for a day or so to dry out.

Almond Paste Poinsettias

Meanwhile take out the almond paste reserved for the decoration. Colour one small piece, about the size of a walnut, bright yellow and divide the remainder in half, colouring one half green and the other red (I use a skewer to drop the colour in, so as not to overdo it). Cut out a template in stiffish paper to the shape of poinsettia leaves (*see* diagram): the red leaves should be about 2¼ inches long and 1 inch wide (5·5 × 2·5 cm) tapering to a point, and the green leaves 3 inches long and 1½ inches wide (7·5 × 4 cm) with a couple of notches on each side.

Roll out both sets of paste to about ⅛ inch (3 mm) thick, then cut out your leaves with the aid of the templates, six red leaves and three green (and perhaps a few in reserve for emergencies), and trace a suggestion of leaf 'veins' on the surface with the back of a knife. Leave the leaves to dry, face upwards over a rolling-pin, then finally model some of the yellow paste into very small pea-sized rounds and leave these to dry overnight.

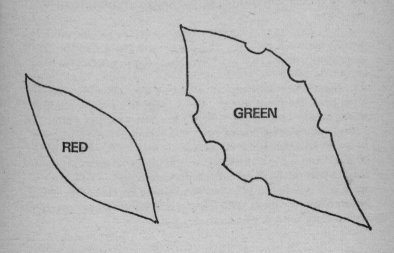

Royal Icing

3 egg whites *plus* 1 extra
Approx 1 lb 2 oz sifted icing sugar (500 g)
1 teaspoon glycerine

Place the egg whites in a completely grease-free bowl, and start stirring in the icing sugar a spoonful at a time until the icing falls thickly from the spoon. At that point stop adding any more sugar and beat as hard as you can for 20 minutes, or until the icing stands up in stiff peaks, then stir in the glycerine. Now spoon half the icing into a screw-top jar, and put aside in the fridge: into the remaining half, beat about 2 teaspoons more of egg white.

Next use a dab of icing to fix the cake to a board, then spread about two-thirds of the remainder on top of the cake. Work the icing back and forth to get rid of any tiny air bubbles, then take a clean (plastic) ruler and holding it at each end glide it to and fro over the surface of the cake until you have a smooth finish. Hold the ruler vertically to remove the excess icing from the top edge of the cake, then spread the remaining icing on to the side of the cake. Keeping your ruler vertical, turn the cake round in one sweep to smooth the sides—a turntable is ideal for this, but two plates set base to base will also do the job. Now leave the cake 24 hours for the icing to dry.

To finish the cake off: mark the centre of the cake with a 3$\frac{1}{4}$-inch (8 cm) plain cutter, or a lid of the same size, then spread the reserved stiff icing on top *outside* this circle. Spike it into snow-like peaks with a broad-bladed knife, and around the edge spike it up then down, to give the effect of hanging snowy icicles! Lastly lay the green paste leaves in the centre of the cake, then the red leaves on top of them and the yellow berries in the centre (fix them in place with a little icing). Set the whole effect off with the red ribbon around the cake, tied in a pretty bow.

Wedding Cake

The last little taste of any wedding celebration is the cake. After everything else, the speeches, toasts and champagne, finally the wedding cake is divided and shared. But oh, so often, beneath those elaborate 'paving-stone' towers a boring mass-produced cake is lurking, and polite nibbles are really all it is fit for. Now a *homemade* wedding cake is something else, because it's actually going to taste delicious.

But, you might protest, you're not really the piping-bag type. Nor am I, but fear not for I have here the instructions for a very pretty, very simple wedding cake. On top of a smooth icing the cake is decorated with flowers made with a special type of modelling icing. There's hardly *any* piping called for at all: the whole thing can easily be made by an amateur.

The first thing you have to do, of course, is decide what size cake you'll need for the number of guests. Four cake sizes in tiers will cover any contingency from 25 to 150: ingredients for 6-inch, 9-inch and 11-inch (15 cm, 23 cm and 28 cm) cakes are given below, and for 8-inch (20 cm) see the Christmas Cake above (the recipe is the same).

Up to 25	One tier	6-inch cake (15 cm)
25–40	One tier	8-inch cake (20 cm)
40–55	One tier	9-inch cake (23 cm)
55–75	One tier	11-inch cake (28 cm)
75–95	Two tiers	8-inch and 9-inch cakes (20 and 23 cm)
95–115	Two tiers	8-inch and 11-inch cakes (20 and 28 cm)
115–130	Two tiers	9-inch and 11-inch cakes (23 and 28 cm)
130–150	Three tiers	6-inch, 9-inch and 11-inch cakes (15, 23 and 28 cm)

*For an 11-inch (28 cm) round Cake or a 10-inch
(25·5 cm) square*

2 lb currants (900 g)
12 oz raisins (350 g)
12 oz sultanas (350 g)
4 oz mixed peel, finely chopped (110 g)
4 oz glacé cherries, rinsed and finely chopped (110 g)

These ingredients should be placed in a bowl the night before
you make the cake, and mixed with 6 tablespoons of brandy.
Cover with a cloth and leave to macerate for at least 12 hours.

1 lb plain flour (450 g)
½ teaspoon salt
1 teaspoon mixed spice
½ teaspoon grated nutmeg
2 dessertspoons black treacle
1 lb soft brown sugar (450 g)
1 lb unsalted butter (450 g)
8 standard eggs
4 oz almonds blanched, peeled and chopped (110 g)
the grated rind of 2 lemons
the grated rind of 2 oranges

First brush an 11-inch (28 cm) round cake tin with melted
butter, and line the base with a circle of greaseproof paper and
the sides with a double thickness of greaseproof (and brush
these with melted butter too). Finally line the base with another
round of greaseproof, and brush with butter.

Pre-heat the oven to gas mark 1 (275 °F) (140 °C)

Start by sieving the flour, salt and spices into a bowl. Then in a
large mixing bowl cream the butter and sugar together until
light and fluffy (most important this is done thoroughly). Then
when the mixture is thoroughly creamed, beat the eggs and add
them, a tablespoonful at a time, beating well after each addition. When all the egg is incorporated, fold in the flour and
spice mixture bit by bit. Then stir in the fruit, nuts and treacle

116

(which will pour more easily if warmed a little first), followed
by the orange and lemon rinds.

Spoon everything into the prepared tin, spreading it evenly
with the back of a tablespoon and making a gentle depression
in the centre. Secure some thick brown paper around the outside of the tin (to protect the edges from the heat), then cover
the top with a square of double greaseproof with a hole in the
centre the size of a 50p piece. Bake on the lower shelf of the
oven (without opening the door) for about 5½ hours. Cool on
a wire rack.

For a 9-inch (23 cm) round Cake or 8-inch (20 cm) square

1 lb 4 oz currants (560 g)
8 oz raisins (225 g)
8 oz sultanas (225 g)
2½ oz mixed peel, finely chopped (60 g)
2½ oz glacé cherries, rinsed and finely chopped (60 g)

All these should be soaked in 4 tablespoons of brandy for at
least 12 hours before you start to make the cake.

10 oz plain flour (275 g)
½ teaspoon salt
¾ teaspoon mixed spice
½ teaspoon grated nutmeg
1 tablespoon black treacle
10 oz soft brown sugar (275 g)
10 oz unsalted butter (275 g)
5 standard eggs
2½ oz almonds blanched, peeled and chopped (60 g)
the grated rind of 1 large orange
the grated rind of 1 large lemon

Prepare a 9-inch (23 cm) round cake tin, and proceed as for the
11-inch (28 cm) cake (above). This one will take about 4¾ hours
to cook.

For a 6-inch (15 cm) Cake (round or square)

8 oz currants (225 g)
3 oz raisins (75 g)
3 oz sultanas (75 g)
1½ oz mixed peel (40 g)
1½ oz glacé cherries (40 g)
1½ oz chopped almonds (40 g)
4 oz plain flour (110 g)
pinch of salt
¼ teaspoon mixed spice
little freshly grated nutmeg

4 oz butter (110 g)
4 oz sugar (110 g)
2 standard eggs
grated rind of ½ orange and ½ lemon
1 rounded teaspoon black treacle

Prepare a 6-inch (15 cm) round cake tin, as above and the cooking time will be approximately 3½ hours.

WEDDING CAKE DECORATION

First Stage

About two weeks before the wedding the cake (or tiers) need to be covered with almond paste, and it must be at least a full week before the icing proper is applied or else the almond paste will tend to discolour the icing.

These quantities are suitable for the above cake sizes round or square.

Almond Paste for 11-inch (28 cm) Cake

1 lb 8 oz ground almonds (675 g)
12 oz icing sugar sifted (350 g)
12 oz caster sugar (350 g)
1 teaspoon almond essence
2 teaspoons lemon juice
2–3 tablespoons sherry
8 egg yolks
apricot jam, warmed

Almond Paste for 9-inch (23 cm) Cake

1 lb ground almonds (450 g)
8 oz caster sugar (225 g)
8 oz icing sugar sifted (225 g)
½ teaspoon almond essence
1 teaspoon lemon juice
1–2 tablespoons sherry
5 egg yolks
apricot jam, warmed

Almond Paste for 6-inch (15 cm) Cake

8 oz ground almonds (225 g)
4 oz caster sugar (110 g)
4 oz icing sugar (110 g)
3 standard egg yolks
½ teaspoon lemon juice
1 dessertspoon sherry
2 drops almond essence
apricot jam, warmed

Mix all the dry ingredients together first, then stir in the essence, lemon juice, sherry and egg yolks and combine everything to form a stiff paste. Now transfer the paste to a pastry board (dusted with icing sugar) and knead it into a ball—without handling it *too* much though since the heat of your hands might make it oily. Before spreading the paste on to the cake, brush the cake all over with some warmed apricot jam. Now take about half the paste and roll it out on a lightly sugared surface to a round approximately 1 inch (2·5 cm) wider than the top of the cake. Then invert the cake on to the paste circle and trim round if you need to.

Next roll the rest of the paste into an oblong half the circumference of the cake and twice the height of the cake (use a tape-measure or piece of string to get these measurements), then cut the oblong in half lengthways. Roll up one strip, lightly place the end on the side of the cake and unroll the paste pressing firmly against the side. Repeat with the other strip to fill the rest of the side of the cake, and press the joins together. Then turn the cake the right way up, even it with a rolling-pin and store in double greaseproof paper for a week before icing.

Royal Icing

If your cake is in tiers, then you'll need *three* layers of hard-set icing—to enable you to balance one on top of the other. If you are only making one tier, one thick layer of icing with the quantities given will be fine, and you can add 2–3 teaspoons of glycerine to give you a softer texture. You will also need cake boards: 14-inch (35 cm) for the 11-inch (28 cm) cake; 11-inch (28 cm) for the 9-inch (23 cm) cake; 10-inch (25·5 cm) for the 8-inch (20 cm) cake; 8-inch (20 cm) for the 6-inch (15 cm) cake. For square cakes always use a board 2 inches larger than the cake. A turntable, palette knife and plastic icing scraper would also be useful.

Note: It's much harder to ice square cakes than round because of the corners!

For 11-inch (28 cm) Cake

2 lb icing sugar (900 g)
6 standard egg whites

For 9-inch (23 cm) Cake

1½ lb icing sugar (700 g)
4 standard egg whites

For 6-inch (15 cm) Cake

1 lb icing sugar (450 g)
2–3 egg whites

Place the egg whites into the largest (grease-free) bowl you have, then stir in the sifted icing sugar with a spoon, two spoonfuls at a time. When the sugar is all stirred in, you can then take an electric mixer and whisk at top speed for 10 minutes, after which time it should be standing up in stiff peaks at least two inches high. As soon as the icing is ready, cover the bowl with a damp cloth to prevent it drying.

Use a little icing to stick the cake on to the board, then give the cake one coat of icing—placing it on the turntable and using about a third of the icing. Ice the top of the cake first, and then the side with the aid of a palette knife. Get the side smooth with a plastic scraper, and the top with a palette knife dipped into hot water and shaken. (A long plastic ruler slid along the top can give a very smooth finish). Smooth the icing right up to the edge of the board too. Store the rest of the icing in a Tupperware container, and leave the cake to dry overnight. Then give it its second and third coats, leaving each coat to dry overnight as well.

Second Stage

Having completed part one of the icing, now comes the most enjoyable stage. I have found that the simpler the design, the better—so I've kept piping to an absolute minimum, and given an idea for a design which includes roses, made with a special modelling icing. The directions for making these roses are illustrated: they're very easy, and if you make two different sizes and group them in clusters all over the cake they look most attractive.

It's a good idea to buy gold or silver braid to fix around the edge of the boards with strong glue, also some gold or silver leaves to tuck in among the roses. And if you wish, you can order a cluster of real flowers from the florist to fix on top of the cake (perhaps to match the bride's bouquet?). Finish off with a band of satin ribbon tied around the circumference of the cake or each tier.

Colour schemes: personally I think an all-white cake isn't as attractive as one with a dash of colour in it. For the first wedding cake I helped to decorate the bride and groom both wore beige and brown—so we matched the cake to them with roses in two different shades of beige, on a white background with gold leaves and braid and a brown satin ribbon around. It certainly looked nicely different from the usual cake design. Then for another wedding, where the bride wore white with pink rosebuds in her bouquet and headdress, we modelled roses in two shades of pink with silver leaves etc, and fresh rosebuds from the florist on top.

Important: if you've decided to make your own wedding cake, do remember to order the proper stand (illustrated, p. 125). These can be hired from bakers' shops, catering firms and hire shops.

Modelling Sugar Paste

2 oz lard (50 g)
2 tablespoons lemon juice
1½ lb sifted icing sugar (700 g)

Food colouring (to be added
with a skewer in *small* drops)

Heat the lard and lemon juice with two tablespoons of water
until the fat melts. Then stir in ½ lb (225 g) of the icing sugar,

and cook over a very low heat until the sugar dissolves and
turns a semi-opaque colour (this takes about two minutes).
Then remove the pan from the heat and stir in the rest of the
sugar which will eventually give you a mixture the consistency
of dough. Turn it out on to a working surface dusted with
sugar, knead for a few seconds, then divide it in half and work
in whatever colours you have chosen. The paste should be
stored in a plastic bag, and when you're ready make up large
roses the size of a 10p piece and small ones the size of old 6d
pieces, then spread them out on a tray to dry overnight (*see*
above). Arrange the roses as you like, with gold leaves here and

there, sticking them on with icing sugar. Around the edges at the base and top pipe a tiny row of beads (with a plain no. 1 writing nozzle). Finally stick the bands of ribbon in place.

NOTES ON DECORATING OTHER CELEBRATION CAKES

Any of these cake recipes, as well as the icing and decorating instructions, can be adapted to suit any other occasion. For a Golden Wedding, for example, two shades of yellow roses, gold leaves and yellow satin ribbon could be used: for a Silver Wedding, pale blue and silver.

Also modelling paste can be used to make other flowers: for a spring birthday, pale green leaves and primroses or blue narcissi flowers. The easiest way is to get hold of a picture of the flower you want to copy.

Important: very deep, dark colours are not possible with this type of paste, as the extra colouring makes the mixture too moist to work. If you want to make, say, a dark-green or red decoration use the modelling type of marzipan (instructions on page 111).

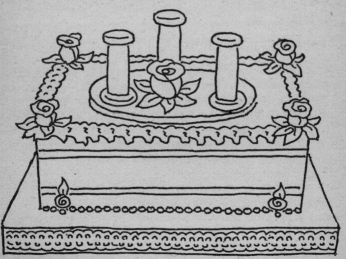

Light Christmas Cake

If you don't like a dark, rich, traditional Christmas cake this one will probably be more suitable—it can be made well in advance, as it keeps well, then iced in the normal way.

8 oz unsalted butter (room temperature) (225 g)
8 oz caster sugar (225 g)
2 oz ground almonds (50 g)
8 oz plain flour, sifted (225 g)
¼ teaspoon salt
4 eggs (standard) at room temperature
3 tablespoons brandy
the grated rinds of 1 orange and 1 lemon
1 tablespoon lemon juice
4 oz walnuts, fairly finely chopped (110 g)
4 oz glacé pineapple (110 g)
4 oz glacé apricots (110 g)
6 oz glacé cherries, rinsed and dried (175 g)
4 oz candied peel (110 g)
2 oz angelica (50 g)
8 oz sultanas (225 g)
2 oz crystallised ginger (50 g)
(All the crystallised fruits need to be chopped up into pieces roughly the size of the sultanas)

Pre-heat the oven to gas mark 3 (325 °F) (170 °C)

The tin for this is an 8-inch (20 cm) one, greased and lined with a double thickness of greaseproof paper.

First put the butter and sugar into the largest mixing bowl you have and beat until the mixture becomes light and fluffy. Then whisk the eggs and add a little at a time to the creamed mixture, beating well between each addition. When all the beaten egg has been added lightly fold in the ground almonds, salt and lemon juice.

Now fold in the brandy, followed by the sifted flour, then the remaining ingredients. Check the recipe carefully to see that you have incorporated all of them into the cake—I usually find it's best to tick everything on a list otherwise you may find, as I once did, a hidden ingredient half way through the cooking time. Next transfer the cake mixture to the tin in tablespoonfuls and level off the top with the back of the spoon. Now tie a band of brown paper around the tin to give extra protection, and place the tin in the oven so the top of it is more or less in the centre. Bake the cake for 1 hour then place a double sheet of greaseproof paper over the top of the tin and turn the heat down to gas mark 2 (300 °F) (150 °C) for a further 2–2¼ hours. When it's cooked it will have begun to shrink away from the sides of the tin and be springy in the centre when you press lightly with your little finger. This cake you can leave in the tin till it's absolutely cold then peel off the papers and wrap it in double greaseproof before storing in the tin.

Glacé Topped Fruit Cake

If you don't like your rich fruit cakes iced, you could use a glacé-fruit topping instead which looks just as festive and attractive.

One 8-inch (20 cm) rich fruit cake (as on page 110)

7 glacé pineapple rings (about 8 oz, 225 g)
12 red glacé cherries (approx)
6 green cherries (approx)
½ oz angelica (approx) (10 g)
6 brazil nuts (approx)
6 walnut halves (approx)
2 tablespoons golden syrup

Warm the syrup in a saucepan to melt it gently, but don't let it boil or it will become too stiff to paint over the cake and fruits. Put the cake on a cake board, and brush it all over with the warmed syrup. Then arrange the pineapple rings (dipped first in the syrup) on top—one in the centre, the others all around it. Now fill the centres of the pineapple rings with cherries, then fill the rest of the space on top of the cake with the remaining fruit and nuts, dipping each piece in the syrup before 'fixing' it to the cake. When you have finished give the whole lot a final brush with syrup. Store in a tin in a cool place.

Easter Simnel Cake

Traditionally a simnel was, strictly speaking, a Mothering Sunday cake, but nowadays it's far more likely to turn up over the Easter weekend.

6 oz butter (175 g)
6 oz caster sugar (175 g)
3 large eggs, beaten
6 oz currants (175 g)
8 oz sultanas (225 g)
2 oz glacé cherries, rinsed, dried, and cut into quarters (50 g)
    the grated rinds of 1 small orange and 1 small lemon
2 oz chopped candied peel (50 g)
8 oz plain flour (225 g)
1 level teaspoon baking powder
1 teaspoon mixed spice
3 tablespoons milk

Then for the topping and filling:
12 oz ground almonds (350 g)
12 oz sieved icing sugar (350 g)
3 large egg yolks
2 teaspoons lemon juice
1 teaspoon almond essence
approx 1 tablespoon brandy or sherry
A dessertspoon apricot jam or redcurrant jelly
1 small egg beaten

Pre-heat the oven to gas mark 2 (300 °F) (150 ° C)

One 8-inch (20 cm) cake tin brushed with melted fat then lined with greaseproof paper, also brushed with fat.

Cream the butter in a bowl, then add the sugar and beat until the mixture is light, pale and fluffy. In a separate bowl beat the eggs together, then add them a little at a time, beating well after each addition so as not to curdle the mixture. When all the eggs are beaten in, take a metal tablespoon and gently fold in the fruits, candied peel and grated orange and lemon rinds. Now sift the flour with the baking powder and mixed spice and then carefully fold it into the mixture alternately with the milk—again use a metal spoon. Don't stir or beat—just fold lightly and carefully until all the flour and the milk have been incorporated. Now spoon half the cake mixture into the prepared tin. Then leave the rest until you've made the almond paste as follows:

Combine 12 oz (350 g), of ground almonds with 12 oz (350 g) sieved icing sugar in a clean bowl, mix them thoroughly together. Then in a jug mix the three egg yolks with the lemon juice and almond essence. Stir this into the almonds and icing sugar and knead to a stiff paste (you may need a little more lemon juice or finish it off with a half to one tablespoon of sherry or brandy). Now take one third of the almond paste, placing the rest in a polythene bag in the fridge, and roll it out —giving it quarter turns as you roll—to form a round approximately 8 inches (20 cm) in diameter (use the cake tin or a circle of paper as a guide). Fit the circle of almond paste over the cake mixture, laying it very gently, then spoon the rest of the mixture over it. Level it out now, then bake the cake in the centre of the oven for about $2\frac{1}{2}$–3 hours, or until the centre is firm and springy.

Leave the cake in the tin to cool for 15 minutes before turning it out on to a wire rack to cool. When it is cool brush the top with a little warmed jam or redcurrant jelly—or failing that egg white will do. Roll out the remaining almond paste and use the cake tin inverted on top to cut out an 8-inch (20 cm) circle, then fit this on top of the cake. Press it securely all round and use a rolling pin to level it as much as possible, then make a criss-cross diamond pattern using the back of the knife. Next make up eleven or twelve little balls of almond paste from the trimmings—these are supposed to represent the apostles so the number depends on whether or not you wish to include poor old Judas. Brush the top of the cake with beaten egg, fix the 'apostles' all round, pressing them gently and brush them with beaten egg too. Then place the cake under a hot grill until the almond paste turns a toasted golden colour. This cake keeps beautifully in an airtight tin so it can be made well in advance.

Ice-Cream Birthday Cake

Children's birthday cakes seem to pop up in all sorts of disguises—houses, space rockets, trains and the like—but what I had never come across was an ice-cream cake. So I thought I'd have a bash and make one for a little 3-year-old friend's birthday. Well, I'm happy to report that the Ice-Cream Birthday Cake was a great success. So here is the recipe, but you'll need to use a deep-freezer or else a small freezer in the top of the fridge (if you don't have either of these you'll have to borrow space in a neighbour's).

1 all-in-one sponge cake (*see* page 34)

1½ litres of ice-cream (three assorted colours) (2⅝ pints)
1½ packets of sponge fingers
1 jelly
¼ pint of double cream (150 ml)
2 tablespoons of jam

A 7-inch (18 cm) round cake tin with a loose base, oiled lightly.

First make up the all-in-one sponge cake recipe on page 34. Then when the sponges are quite cold, carefully slice each one in half horizontally—so you have four layers of sponge altogether. Now fit one layer into the base of the prepared cake tin, then spoon ½ litre (⅞ pint) of one colour ice-cream all over it, spreading it out evenly. Then, working quickly, fit another sponge layer on top—then a second layer of ice-cream, another sponge, a third layer of ice cream and finally the last sponge.

Now quickly cover the top of the tin with foil and place the cake in the freezer and freeze overnight. Next day make up the jelly, dissolving it in ½ pint (275 ml) of hot water (it needs to be fairly stiff so don't use any more water). Cool the jelly until it's syrupy and about to set, then take the cake out of the freezer and spoon the jelly all over the surface—where it will start to set almost immediately. Don't worry if any jelly seeps down the sides, it won't show later.

Return the cake to the freezer, covered again with foil. Store in the freezer, not longer than a month. Then to serve, take it out about an hour before serving and have ready ¼ pint (150 ml) of whipped cream and a piping bag fitted with a small star nozzle and some jam. Hold a hot dishcloth round the tin for a few seconds, then, ease the tin gently upwards, slide a palette knife underneath and transfer the cake from the base on to a plate. Now spread the non-sugared sides of the sponge fingers with jam and position them vertically all round the side of the cake. On top, pipe rosettes of cream all around the inside edge, and in the centre pipe the figure of the child's age. Then return the cake to the refrigerator. Just before serving decorate with candles and tie a coloured ribbon around the centre with a large bow, then light the candles before carrying the cake to the table.

Note: You can make this look really attractive by using a red jelly on top with pink candles and pink ribbon—or a lemon jelly and yellow ribbon etc. The best way to cope with the ribbon and bow at the last minute would be to have ready a length of wide ribbon measuring the exact circumference of the cake, with a ready-made bow at one end, then simply pin it into position before the cake goes to the table. After the candles have been blown out, you can unpin it very easily and perhaps save it for next year!

Traditional Oatmeal Parkin

Real oatmeal parkin is unbeatable, but *do* make sure you leave it at least a week before eating—that way it will become much more moist and sticky than when it was first cooked. Originally it was kept in proper wooden parkin boxes, but nowadays a tin will do instead.

½ lb medium oatmeal (available at wholefood shops) (225 g)
¼ lb self-raising flour (110 g)
1 pinch of salt
7 oz golden syrup (200 g)
1 oz (25 g) *plus* 1 teaspoon black treacle
¼ lb margarine (110 g)
¼ lb soft brown sugar (110 g)
2 teaspoons ground ginger
1 large egg, beaten
1 tablespoon milk

Pre-heat the oven to gas mark 1 (275 °F) (140 °C)

One 8-inch (20 cm) square cake tin, lightly greased
First weigh a saucepan on the scales, and weigh the syrup and treacle into it. Then add the margarine and the sugar to the saucepan and place it over a gentle heat until the margarine has melted down—don't go away and leave it unattended, because for this you don't want it to boil. Meanwhile measure the oatmeal, flour and ginger into a mixing bowl, add a pinch of salt, then gradually stir in the warmed syrup mixture till the mixture is all thoroughly blended. Next add the beaten egg, and lastly the milk. Now pour the mixture into the prepared tin and bake on the centre shelf of the oven for 1¾–2 hours. Then cool the parkin in the tin for 30 minutes before turning out. Don't worry too much if the parkin sinks slightly in the middle—it sometimes happens in Yorkshire too, I'm told.

With the disappearance of the corner cake shop and the advent of bulk factory baking, it's the little cakes that have suffered most. How many times have you looked in the window of one of a large chain of bakers' shops stacked with cakes, and not really seen anything that you'd like to buy?

The proverbial synthetic cream horn lives on and on, but what happened to the real cakes of my childhood—sticky currant buns, Chelsea buns, real chocolate éclairs, proper Eccles cakes? Well, with campaigns for 'real' things springing up on all sides, it's not too surprising to find there's actually been a campaign in the north of England for real Eccles cakes. Their champions, it seems, are fed up with stale cake crumbs being used to eke out the vanishing fruit, and the pastry, they say, is definitely not what it used to be. I do hope mine pass for real: they certainly taste good.

In short, if it's little cakes you want, my advice is to make them yourself. They're so useful for lunch-boxes, picnics or car journeys. And if, like me, you tend to get roped in on the Cricket Teas rota, it's often quicker (and definitely cheaper) to make your own instead of traipsing round trying to buy some.

Eccles Cakes

(Makes about 2 dozen)

These famous little English cakes are one of my mother's specialities, and this is her recipe.

For the Quick Flaky Pastry:
8 oz plain flour (225 g)
6 oz margarine (175 g)
1 good pinch of salt
cold water, to mix

For the filling:
3 oz butter (75 g)
5 oz soft brown sugar (150 g)
5 oz currants (150 g)
1 teaspoon cinnamon
½ teaspoon freshly grated nutmeg
the grated rind of 1 large orange
2 oz finely chopped peel (50 g)

To finish off: milk and caster sugar

To make the pastry, weigh the margarine (hard from the refrigerator), then wrap it in a piece of foil and place it in the freezing compartment of the fridge for half an hour. Meanwhile sift the flour and salt into a bowl, then when you take the margarine out of the freezer hold it with the foil, dip it into the flour, then grate it on a coarse grater placed in the bowl over the flour. Carry on dipping the margarine down into the flour to make it easier to grate. When you have finished you will have a lump of grated margarine sitting in the middle of the flour. Then take a palette knife and start to cut the fat into the flour (don't use your hands) until the mixture is crumbly. Now add enough water so that it forms a dough that leaves the bowl clean (you *can* use your hands for the dough), then place it in a polythene bag and chill it in the main part of the refrigerator for half an hour.

Meanwhile prepare the filling by first melting the butter in a small saucepan. Then take it off the heat and stir in all the filling ingredients quite thoroughly and leave it to cool. Next turn the dough out on to a lightly floured surface. Roll it out to about ⅛ inch (3 mm) thick, then using a plain 3¼-inch (8 cm) cutter, cut the pastry into rounds. Put a teaspoon of filling on to each round, then brush the edge of half the circle of pastry with water, and bring the other side up and seal it. Then bring the corners up to the centre, and pinch to seal well. Now turn your sealed pastry parcel over, so that the seam is underneath, then gently roll the whole thing to flatten it to about ¼ inch thick (½ cm), and pat it into a round shape. Place them all on a greased baking sheet and gash each cake diagonally across three times, using a sharp knife. Now brush them with milk and sprinkle with caster sugar, and bake them in the oven pre-heated to gas mark 7 (425 °F) (220 °C) for about 15 minutes or until golden-brown. Then transfer them to a wire rack to cool.

Orange Butterfly Cakes   (Makes about 13)

These are filled with orange curd, instead of lemon, for a change. Alternatively they're very nice filled with plain whipped cream—or whipped cream flavoured with coffee.

For the cakes:
6 oz self-raising flour (175 g)
pinch of salt
4 oz soft margarine (at room temperature) (110 g)
4 oz caster sugar (110 g)
2 large eggs
1 dessertspoon orange juice
grated rind of 1 orange

For the curd filling:
finely grated rind and juice of 1 orange (small)
juice of ½ lemon
1½ oz caster sugar (40 g)
2 large eggs
2 oz unsalted butter (50 g)

Pre-heat the oven to gas mark 5 (375 °F) (190 °C)

A greased patty tin and paper baking cases.

Start by making the filling. Put the first four ingredients for the curd in a bowl and whisk together. Then add the butter, cut into lumps, and fit the bowl over a pan of simmering water. Now take a wooden spoon and stir continuously until the curd thickens—about 10 minutes. Then remove the bowl and leave the curd to get quite cold. To make the cakes combine all the ingredients together in a bowl and beat until absolutely smooth —1–2 minutes. Then drop an equal quantity of the mixture into the paper cases. Tap the tin two or three times to settle the cake mix, then bake on the shelf just above the centre for 15–20 minutes or until the cakes are well risen and golden. Then remove them to a wire rack and leave to cool.

Then angle a small sharp knife and cut to within about ½ inch (1 cm) of the edge of each cake to remove a cone-shaped round, leaving a cavity in the centre. Cut the round in half and set aside. Now fill the centre of each cake with the curd and return the two pieces of cake to sit on top like butterfly wings.

Viennese Tartlets (Makes about 16)

These are very short little cakes with a nice crumbly texture also, as they require no eggs, they're good for those on low cholesterol diet.

7 oz self-raising flour (200 g)
8 oz margarine or butter (225 g)
3 oz icing sugar, sifted (75 g)
2 oz cornflour (50 g)
a little red jam
icing sugar
paper cake cases

You'll also need a large nylon piping bag fiitted with a large rosette nozzle.

Pre-heat the oven to gas mark 4 (350 °F) (180 °C)

First place the paper cases in some patty tins ready.

Then beat the fat and icing sugar together until very soft and creamy and afterwards stir in the sieved flour and cornflour to form a soft paste. Now sit the piping bag in an empty jug—nozzle end down—and fold the ends of the piping bag all round the edge of the jug. This leaves you with two hands free to transfer the paste to the piping bag. When it's all in, squeeze the paste down the bag to the nozzle and pipe a circle of paste in the base of each paper case. You'll need to scrape the paste down the bag once or twice during piping, and to do this simply lay the bag down flat on the working surface and use a stiff plastic spatula or palette knife to push the mixture inside towards the nozzle end. Then carry on piping. Bake the cakes for 20–25 minutes or until golden brown but they will still be just slightly soft in the centre so don't worry about that. Remove them from the patty tins to a wire rack to cool for 15 minutes, leaving them in their paper cases. Now put a spot of red jam—barely the size of a ½p piece—in the centre of each tartlet, then sift a light dusting of icing sugar over the top of each one and leave them to cool. It doesn't matter if the icing sugar obscures the jam—it will soon be absorbed by the jam so you'll end up with delicious little red blobs in the centre. Store these in an airtight tin.

Chocolate Choux Buns   (Makes 9)

These lovely light, airy choux pastry buns are filled and topped with a squidgy chocolate mousse mixture and a final coating of chopped nuts.

For the pastry:
2½ oz strong flour (60 g)
2 oz butter, cut in small pieces (50 g)
1 teaspoon sugar
2 standard eggs, well beaten
¼ pint water (150 ml)

For the filling:
6 oz plain chocolate (175 g)
3 large eggs, separated

For the topping:
Chopped, toasted hazelnuts

Make the filling several hours in advance. Melt the chocolate in a heat-proof bowl set over a pan of barely simmering water. Then beat the egg yolks into the chocolate and allow the mixture to cool. Now whisk the egg whites to the soft peak stage. Stir one tablespoon of egg white into the chocolate mixture to loosen it then carefully fold in the rest of the egg white. Cover the bowl and chill in a refrigerator for about 3 hours. Now for the choux pastry. *Pre-heat the oven to gas mark 6, (400 °F) (200 °C)* and you'll need a lightly greased baking sheet. In all my experiments with choux pastry I've found that 'strong' flour gives the best results. However, if you haven't got any strong flour handy, ordinary plain flour will do. Choux pastry is quite different from any other sort of pastry but it is extremely easy to make once you've practised a couple of times. Start by placing the water in a saucepan with the pieces of butter and the sugar and bring this up to the boil. While that's happening, sift the flour on to a piece of greaseproof paper. As soon as the mixture has come to the boil and the butter has melted, make a fold in the paper, turn the heat off and 'shoot' the flour into the pan, stirring vigorously until you get a small ball of paste. This happens very quickly—in less than a minute. Now gradually add the eggs a little at a time, beating vigorously until all the eggs have been added and the mixture is smooth and glossy. (I do all this with an electric hand-whisk, switched to medium speed, but a wooden spoon and a bit more elbow grease will do.)

Next, quickly run the greased baking sheet under a cold tap, then tap it to get rid of the excess water and place rough dessertspoonsful of choux paste—about 9 in all—on to the baking sheet. The moisture, by the way, will create a steamy atmosphere which will help the choux buns to rise. Now place them on a high shelf in the oven and after 10 minutes increase the heat to gas mark 7 (425 °F) (220 °C) and give them another 20 minutes cooking, by which time they'll be beautifully puffy and crisp. Remove them from the baking sheet straight away on to a cooling tray and pierce the side of each one with a small sharp knife or a skewer, which will let out the air inside and prevent them going soggy.

It's best not to put in the filling until about an hour before serving. All you do is slice the choux buns horizontally, but not quite in half, then place a spoonful of the mousse inside, spread a little over the top using the back of the spoon and, finally, sprinkle each one with chopped hazelnuts.

Note: If you want to make profiteroles, divide the choux paste into teaspoonfuls, give them slightly less cooking time and then, to serve, fill with whipped cream and pour hot chocolate sauce over as they go to the table.

Coffee Eclairs

I think these are very elegant for a rather special afternoon tea.

Choux pastry as above

For the filling:
½-pint double cream (275 ml)
1 tablespoon instant coffee
1 level tablespoon caster sugar

For the icing:
5 oz sieved icing sugar (150 g)
2 teaspoons instant coffee

Pre-heat the oven to gas mark 6 (400 °F) (200 °C)

Make the choux pastry then spoon it into a large nylon piping bag, fitted with a plain ½-inch (1 cm) piping nozzle. Pipe the mixture on to rinsed baking sheets (as above) in lengths just over 3 inches (7.5 cm) long. These will probably seem a little too long before baking but the mixture contracts quite a lot as it rises so it will be all right. Bake the éclairs on a high shelf for 10 minutes, then increase the heat to gas mark 7 (425 °F) (220 °C) for a further 10 minutes. Remove them from the oven to a wire cooling tray and make a slight hole in the side of each one.

For the filling, dissolve the coffee and sugar in 2 teaspoons of boiling water. Then beat the cream till thickened and add the coffee mixture to it, stirring to blend it evenly. Now wash and dry the piping bag thoroughly; spoon the coffee cream into it, using the same nozzle. Slit the éclairs along one side, pipe in the cream then carefully lift the tops gently back over the cream.

Next prepare the icing. In a small basin dissolve the coffee in a tablespoon of boiling water, then sift the icing sugar into it and stir. It should now be the consistency of thick cream. Finally, dip the tops of the éclairs into the icing and let the excess drip back into the bowl before returning each one to the wire rack.

Madeleines
(Makes approximately 10)

For these traditional little French cakes you'll need special tins called dariole moulds—available at good kitchen equipment shops.

2 standard eggs, beaten
4 oz butter or margarine (110 g)
4 oz caster sugar (110 g)
4 oz self-raising flour (110 g)
¼ teaspoon vanilla essence
About 5 glacé cherries, halved
About half a 12-oz jar red jam (350 g)
About 4 oz blanched almonds (110 g) (or desiccated coconut)

Pre-heat the oven to gas mark 5 (375 °F) (190 °C)

Brush about ten dariole moulds with melted fat and dust with flour.

Cream the fat and sugar together until light and fluffy and

gradually beat in the eggs, a little at a time. Then add the vanilla essence before gently folding in the flour. Now half fill each dariole mould with the cake mixture. Because these tins are rather small they tend to slip sideways through the rods of the shelves in the oven. To prevent this, place a wire rack on top of the oven shelf and arrange the dariole moulds on this. Then bake for about 15 minutes, or until springy to the touch. Leave them in the tins for one minute then turn them out on to a wire rack and, when they're cool, you may need to trim the bases a bit so that they stand up. Then put the jam in a saucepan with a tablespoon of water and heat gently, stirring occasionally, before rubbing it through a nylon sieve into a bowl. Spear each madeleine at the base with a fork, then hold it over the bowl while you brush all round it with the jam.

Have the almonds, ready chopped, (or the coconut) on a plate beside you. Roll the madeleines in the nuts and leave to firm up on the wire rack. Lastly, put a tiny dab of jam on the base of each half of glacé cherry and use to decorate the top of each cake.

Spiced Apple and Sultana Fingers

This is a good recipe to make when the windfall apples are demanding attention in the autumn.

For the pastry:
8 oz butter (225 g)
2 oz caster sugar (50 g)
1 egg
12 oz plain flour (350 g)

For the filling:
1 level tablespoon cornflour
2 level tablespoons dark brown sugar
¾ teaspoons mixed spice
4 oz sultanas (110 g)
1 large cooking apple, peeled, cored and finely chopped

1 teaspoon lemon juice
a little icing sugar

Pre-heat the oven to gas mark 6 (400 °F) (200 °C)

First cream the butter and sugar until light and fluffy. Then
lightly beat the egg, and beat it a little at a time into the creamed
butter, then gradually work in the flour. Now place half of this
paste in a greased Swiss roll tin (about 13 × 9 inches) (33 × 23
cm) and press it out all over the base of the tin with your hands,
then put the other half of the pastry in a polythene bag in the
refrigerator. Take a saucepan and in it mix the cornflour, sugar
and spice, and gradually blend in ¼ pint (150 ml) of water,
followed by the sultanas, chopped apple and lemon juice.
Bring the mixture slowly to the boil, then simmer very gently
for 3 minutes, remove the pan from the heat and allow the
mixture to cool. When it's cool enough, spread it carefully and
evenly over the pastry base. Now roll out the remaining pastry
on a lightly floured board to the size of the tin, and cover the
apple filling with it, pressing lightly round the edges to seal.
Now into the oven with it for 20–25 minutes, or until the
pastry is lightly golden. Then dust with icing sugar and leave
to cool in the tin before cutting into fingers.

Crusty Currant Cakes   (Makes 15 squares)

So named because they have a delicious curranty crusted topping.

12 oz margarine (350 g)
12 oz caster sugar (350 g)
3 eggs (standard) beaten
½ teaspoon vanilla essence
6 oz plain flour (175 g)
7 oz currants (200 g)
2 oz blanched almonds, finely chopped (50 g)
2 oz icing sugar, sifted (50 g)
squeeze of lemon juice

Pre-heat the oven to gas mark 4 (350 °F) (180 °C)

Begin by brushing a large Swiss roll tin, 13 × 9 inches (33 × 23 cm) with melted fat. Then line it with silicone paper to stand up about 1 inch (2·5 cm) above the rim of the tin.

Now cream the margarine and sugar together until pale, light and fluffy. Gradually beat in the eggs, a little at a time, beating well between each addition to prevent any curdling. Next fold in the vanilla essence, followed by the flour, then spread the mixture evenly in the prepared tin. Now combine the currants and almonds together in a basin and sprinkle these evenly over the surface of the cake mixture. Bake for about 40–45 minutes. If the cake looks as though it might be over-browned by the time it's cooked, cover it with a sheet of greaseproof paper and continue cooking. It's done when it feels fairly firm in the centre. Let the cake cool in the tin. Then lift it out by holding on to the paper and transfer it to a board or work surface.

Now blend the icing sugar with a squeeze of lemon juice and a few drops of water to a 'thinnish' pouring consistency and, taking a teaspoon of the icing at a time, drop a thin stream of icing on to the cake, wandering over the cake at random to form squiggly lines, then leave the icing to set.

Cut the cake into squares using a sharp knife and separate the slices carefully from the lining paper—one at a time—with the aid of a palette knife. Store the cakes in a tin.

Gingerbread Men   (Makes about 20)

This very well-behaved dough can put up with quite a bit of punishment and is, therefore, ideal for children to play around with. You can sometimes buy proper cutters for making 'men' but, if not, you can easily make a template out of stiff card and cut around it.

3 oz soft brown sugar, sieved (75 g)
2 tablespoons golden syrup
1 tablespoon black treacle
1 tablespoon water
3½ oz butter or margarine (95 g)

1 teaspoon cinnamon
1 teaspoon ginger
1 pinch ground cloves
finely grated rind of ½ an orange
½ teaspoon bicarbonate of soda
about 8 oz plain flour (225 g)

Lightly greased baking sheets.

Put the sugar, syrup, treacle, water, spices and rind together in a large saucepan. Then bring them to boiling point, stirring all the time. Now remove the pan from the heat and stir in the fat, cut into lumps, and the bicarbonate of soda. Next stir in the flour gradually until you have a smooth manageable dough —add a little more flour if you think it needs it. Now leave the dough—covered—in a cool place to become firm, approximately 30 minutes.

Pre-heat the oven to gas mark 4 (350 °F) (180 °C)

Now roll the dough out on a lightly floured surface to ⅛ inch (3 mm) thick and cut out the gingerbread men. Currants can be pressed into the dough to simulate eyes, noses, mouths and buttons down their fronts. Arrange them on the lightly greased baking sheets and bake for 10–15 minutes or until the biscuits feel firm when lightly pressed with a finger tip. Leave the biscuits to cool on the baking sheets for a few minutes before transferring them to a wire rack.

For a children's party, instead of arranging currants along the bodies, leave them plain then afterwards pipe on in icing the name of each child.

Spiced Date Crunchies

(Makes about 18)

The semolina in this recipe gives these little biscuits a lovely short crunchy texture.

6 oz self raising flour (175 g)
6 oz semolina (175 g)
6 oz butter (175 g)
3 oz demerara sugar (75 g)
½ lb dates, stoned and chopped (225 g)
1 tablespoon dark brown sugar
4 tablespoons water
1 tablespoon lemon juice
½ teaspoon cinnamon powder

Pre-heat the oven to gas mark 5 (375 °F) (190 °C)

First grease a small Swiss roll tin, measuring 8 × 12 inches (20 × 30 cm).

Then put the chopped dates, brown sugar, water, lemon juice and cinnamon in a small saucepan and heat gently stirring occasionally, until the mixture looks as though it will spread fairly easily. Then take the saucepan off the heat and leave it to cool. While it's cooling, mix the flour and semolina together in a bowl.

Then place the butter and sugar together in another small saucepan and heat gently until the butter has completely melted, now stir this mixture into the flour and semolina. Mix well, then press half the mixture into the greased tin using your hands. Spread the date mixture carefully over the surface then top with the remaining flour and semolina mixture; this will by now have cooled a little and will probably be a bit crumbly, so just sprinkle it over the date mixture and fork it over lightly. Now bake for 25–30 minutes on a centre shelf until the surface is tinged a nice golden colour. Then cool, cut into bars and serve, or store in a tin till needed.

Good Old Rock Cakes (Makes 10–12)

Everyone, whatever their age, seems to love good old rock
cakes. I like these made with half wholewheat and half plain
white flour, but you can use all white if you prefer.

6 oz wholewheat flour (175 g)
6 oz plain white flour (175 g)
¼ teaspoon salt
2 teaspoons baking powder
about ¼ of a freshly grated nutmeg
¼ teaspoon mixed spice
6 oz butter or margarine (175 g)
6 oz soft brown sugar (175 g)
3 oz currants (75 g)
1 oz chopped peel (25 g)
1 egg
1–2 tablespoons milk

Pre-heat the oven to gas mark 5 (375 °F) (190 °C)

One large, or two small baking sheets, well greased.

Mix the flour, salt, baking powder and sugar in a bowl, making sure you get all the little lumps out of the sugar, then add
the spices and rub in the butter (or margarine) until the mixture
looks like fine breadcrumbs and, lastly, stir in the fruit. Now
break the egg into a separate bowl and whisk it lightly with a
fork, then add it to the flour mixture. Stir until the mixture
forms a stiff dough (you may need to add a tablespoon of
milk, though certainly not more than two—or they might turn
out a little too 'rocky'). Now, using two forks, pile the mixture
in irregular spiky heaps on greased baking sheets. Bake for
15–20 minutes or until golden-brown and firm, then leave to
cool off for a minute on the trays before removing to a wire
rack.

Spicy Hot Cross Buns (Makes about 12)

If you've been denying yourself through Lent, what better treat could you have at the end of it than a plate of sticky buns —still warm from the oven and spread with lots of butter?

1 lb plain flour (450 g)
1 teaspoon caster sugar
1½–2 fl oz warmed milk (40–50 ml)
1 level teaspoon salt
2 oz cut mixed peel (50 g)
2 oz butter (melted) (50 g)
¼ pint hand-hot water (150 ml)
1 level tablespoon dried yeast
1 rounded teaspoon mixed spice
3 oz currants (75 g)
2 oz caster sugar (50 g)
1 egg beaten

For the glaze:
2 tablespoons granulated sugar
2 tablespoons water

Pre-heat the oven to gas mark 7 (425 °F) (220 °C)

A greased baking sheet.

First stir 1 teaspoon of caster sugar into the ¼ pint (150 ml) of hand-hot water, then sprinkle in the dried yeast and leave it till a good frothy 'beer' head forms. Meanwhile sift the flour, salt and mixed spice into a mixing bowl and add the sugar, currants and mixed peel. Then make a well in the centre, pour in the yeast mixture plus 1½ fl oz (40 ml) of milk (again, hand-hot), the beaten egg and the melted butter. Now mix it to a dough, starting with a wooden spoon and finishing with your hands (add a spot more milk if it needs it). Then transfer the dough on to a clean surface and knead it until it feels smooth and elastic—about 6 minutes. Now pop it back into the bowl, cover the bowl with a lightly oiled plastic bag (a pedal-bin liner is ideal), and leave it in a warm place to rise—it will take about an hour to double its original size. Then turn it out and knead it again, back down to its original size. Divide the mixture into twelve round portions, arrange them on the greased baking sheet (allowing plenty of room for expansion), and make a deep cross in each one with a sharp knife. Leave them to rise once more, covering again with the oiled polythene bag—they should take about 25 minutes. Then bake the buns for about 15 minutes. Then, while they're cooking, melt the sugar and water over a gentle heat, and brush the buns with it as soon as they come out of the oven to make them nice and sticky.

Chelsea Buns (Makes 9 buns)

I loved these iced curranty buns when I was a child and took great delight in uncurling them with each mouthful.

8 oz plain white flour (225 g)
½ teaspoon salt
2 teaspoons dried yeast
1 teaspoon sugar
1 egg, beaten
1 oz butter or margarine (25 g)
1½ fl oz cold milk
1½ fl oz boiling water

For the filling:
2 oz soft butter (50 g)
2 oz soft brown sugar (50 g)
2 oz currants (50 g)
2 oz sultanas (50 g)
1 oz cut mixed peel (25 g)
1 teaspoon mixed spice

Then to glaze:
3 oz icing sugar, sifted (75 g)
Water to mix to a thin glaze

A 9-inch (23 cm) cake tin, well greased.

First measure the cold milk in a measuring jug and add the boiling water. Then whisk in the sugar and yeast and leave it

149

to froth for 10 minutes. Meanwhile sift the flour and salt into a bowl and rub in the fat. Then pour in the beaten egg and frothed yeast and mix to a non-sticky dough. If it seems a little dry, add a teaspoon or two more of warm water. Now turn the dough out on to a lightly floured surface and knead for 10 minutes or until the dough shows slight blisters just under the surface. Then return it to the bowl, cover with clingfilm, and leave it in a warm place until doubled in bulk—about 45 minutes to 1 hour depending on the warmth.

Then turn the dough out and punch it down and knead to disperse any large air bubbles. Now roll it out to an oblong, roughly 12 × 9 inches (30 × 23 cm). Then spread the butter all over and sprinkle with the sugar, fruit and spice. Now roll it up lengthways (i.e. from the long side) then slice the roll up into nine pieces and arrange these pieces in the cake tin, putting eight buns in a circle and the ninth in the middle. Then set them aside in a warm place to prove for about 30 to 45 minutes by which time they will have expanded, joined up and filled up all the space. Now bake them at gas mark 5 (375 °F) (190 °C) for 30 minutes. Then cool for 10 minutes and remove them from the tin in one piece.

To finish off, paint all over the surface with a thin glacé icing and pull them apart as you serve them.

Welsh Cakes

My Welsh mother-in-law sometimes makes these delicious little cakes to cheer up my husband and father-in-law on a Saturday afternoon after losing a football match.

8 oz self-raising flour (225 g)
4 oz butter or margarine (110 g)
3 oz mixed fruit or just sultanas (75 g)
3 oz caster sugar (75 g)
1 large egg
½ teaspoon mixed spice

To cook these you really need the traditional heavy, flat, iron pan (sometimes called a griddle or a girdle). However, a good solid heavy frying pan, with a flat base, will do.

First, sift the dry ingredients together, then rub in the butter or margarine as you would if you were making pastry. Then, when the mixture becomes crumbly, add the fruit and mix it in thoroughly. Then beat the egg lightly and add it to the mixture. Mix to a dough and, if the mixture seems a little too dry, add just a spot of milk. Now transfer the dough on to a lightly floured working surface and roll it out to about $\frac{1}{4}$ inch (5 mm) thick. Then, using a $2\frac{1}{2}$-inch (6·5 cm) plain cutter, cut the dough into rounds, re-rolling the trimmings until all the dough is used. Next, lightly grease the thick heavy pan, using a piece of kitchen paper smeared with lard. Now heat the pan over a medium heat and cook the Welsh cakes for about 3 minutes each side. If they look as if they're browning too quickly, turn the heat down a bit because it's important to cook them through —but they should be fairly brown and crisp on the outside. Serve them warm, with lots of butter and home-made jam or perhaps some Welsh honey.

Doughnuts

If you're very thin and have no weight problems, you can make some of these. If, like me, you feel fat just thinking about them perhaps you better not.

8 oz plain white flour (225 g)
1½ oz caster sugar (40 g)
2 teaspoons dried yeast
1 egg, beaten
1 oz butter or margarine (25 g)
½ teaspoon salt
3 tablespoons milk
3 tablespoons boiling water

For the filling:
red jam

For the coating:
2 oz caster sugar (50 g)
1 teaspoon cinnamon

Oil for frying

First measure the milk into a measuring jug, and then add the boiling water, a teaspoon of the sugar and the yeast. Then stir and leave the jug in a warm place for about 10 minutes till the yeast mixture is frothy. Now put the rest of the sugar, the salt and the flour into a bowl and rub in the fat. Then pour in the beaten egg and the frothy yeast and stir and mix to a smooth dough. If it seems a little dry, sprinkle in another teaspoon or so of warm water. Now turn the dough on to a lightly floured surface and knead it for about 10 minutes by which time it should feel springy and show slight blisters just under the surface. Return it to the bowl, cover with clingfilm or a cloth, and leave it in a warm place to rise until double in size (this takes about 45 minutes to 1 hour). When it has risen tip the dough out on to the working surface again, punch it down and knead it again to disperse any large air bubbles. Now divide the dough into eight equal pieces and flatten out each piece to a round disc shape. Then put about half a teaspoon of jam in the centre of each one, then bring the edges up and pinch them together so you have a soft ball of dough with some jam inside. Now place them either on one large or two small greased baking sheets and enclose them in a large lightly oiled plastic bag (bin liner). Then put them back in a warm place to rise again for about 30 minutes or until they've doubled in size. Now heat a pan of deep oil (a flavourless groundnut oil is best). If you have a cooking thermometer, which is advisable, the temperature should be about 370 °F (185 °C). Fry the doughnuts about three at a time, turning them frequently so that they will brown evenly. Altogether they'll need about 4 minutes frying time. Drain them on crumpled kitchen paper, then toss them in the combined cinnamon and sugar and it's important to eat them on the same day.

SCONES, CRUMPETS AND MUFFINS

Isn't it a pity that once again our traditional recipes for such delicious things as crumpets or muffins have been totally eclipsed by the pre-packed versions? And yet homemade they can provide a real taste of luxury at very little cost.

Homemade Crumpets   (Makes 12)

You used to be able to buy proper metal crumpet rings for making these but, as they're hard to get hold of nowadays, I make mine with egg cooking rings, which are just as good.

½ lb strong plain flour (225 g)
1 level teaspoon salt
1 level tablespoon dried yeast
1 teaspoon caster sugar
½ pint milk (275 ml)
2 fl oz water (55 ml)

One thick-based frying pan and a little lard.

Heat the milk and water together in a small saucepan to 'hand hot'. Then pour it into a jug, stir in the sugar and dried yeast and leave it in a warm place for 10–15 minutes to get a really good frothy head. While that's happening sift the flour and salt into a mixing bowl, make a well in the centre then, when the yeast mixture is frothy, pour it all in. Now, with a wooden spoon, gradually work the flour into the liquid, beating very well at the end to make a perfectly smooth batter. Cover the basin with a folded tea towel and leave it in a warm place for about 45 minutes. By that time, it will have become very light and frothy-looking and you can start to cook the crumpets. First, thoroughly grease the insides of the egg rings, then grease the frying pan with lard too, place it over a medium heat and arrange the rings in it. Then, when the pan is hot, spoon one tablespoon of the crumpet mixture into each ring, and let them cook for about 4 or 5 minutes. It's fascinating watching them cook—lots of tiny little bubbles appear on the surface and then they suddenly all start to burst leaving the traditional holes. Now take a large spoon and fork, turn the crumpets over and lift off the rings. If they tend to stick—using a tea towel to protect your hands—give them a little push through the rings. Cook the crumpets for another minute. Then to serve, butter the crumpets generously on the sides with the holes. The cooled rings can be re-greased for the next batch and, if you want to make them well in advance, toast them lightly on both sides before serving.

English Muffins (Makes 12)

Now here's a neglected delicacy—real old-fashioned muffins. They're very welcoming served for tea on a chilly day.

1 lb strong plain flour (450 g)
1 rounded teaspoon salt
8 fl oz milk (225 ml)
2 fl oz water (55 ml)

1 teaspoon caster sugar
2 level teaspoons dried yeast

A thick solid-based frying pan or a girdle and some lard.

Measure the milk and water in a small saucepan and heat until just 'hand hot' i.e. so that you can hold your little finger in without it burning. Now pour it into a jug, add the sugar and dried yeast, mix it with a fork and leave it for about 10 minutes to get a real frothy head.

Meanwhile sift the flour and salt into a large mixing bowl, making a well in the centre, then pour in the frothy yeast mixture and mix it to a soft dough—it should leave the bowl cleanly but if it seems a bit sticky add a spot more flour. On the other hand if it seems a little dry add just a spot more water. Now transfer the dough to a flat surface and knead it for about 10 minutes by which time it should be very smooth and elastic. The dough can go back into the bowl now. Just slip the bowl inside a large polythene bag (a transparent pedal bin liner is ideal), and leave it in a warm place until the dough has doubled in size. This will take about 45 minutes or longer, depending on the temperature. When the dough has risen, lightly flour the work surface, then tip the dough out and roll it out to about ½ inch (1 cm) thick, then using a 3-inch (7·5 cm plain cutter cut out twelve rounds, re-rolling the dough a couple of times again if it starts to get puffy. Mix the scraps and re-roll as well to use it all up. Now place the muffins on an ungreased lightly floured baking sheet, sprinkling them with a little more flour, then leave them to puff up again for about 25–35 minutes in a warm place. When they are ready to be cooked, grease a thick-based frying pan or girdle with just a trace of lard, then heat the pan over a medium heat, add some muffins and cook them for about 7 minutes on each side, turning the heat down to low as soon as they go in. You'll need to do this in three or four batches but they can be made well in advance.

If you want to serve them in the traditional way all you do is break them just a little around their waists without opening them, then toast them lightly on both sides. The correct way to eat them is just to pull them apart without cutting and insert

155

a lot of butter. You can store them in an airtight tin for about two days before toasting if you have any left over.

Devonshire Scones

(Makes approximately 12 scones)

What could be more English than clotted cream, homemade strawberry jam, and freshly made scones—slightly crisp on the outside and light and soft within?

8 oz self-raising flour, sieved (225 g)
1½ oz butter or margarine (room temperature) (40 g)
¼ pint milk (150 ml)
1½ level tablespoons caster sugar
pinch of salt
1 small (4 oz) (100 ml) carton clotted cream, or ¼ pint double
  (150 ml) cream whipped
strawberry jam

Pre-heat the oven to gas mark 7 (425 °F) (220 °C)

A greased baking tin.

Begin by rubbing the butter into the sieved flour quickly, using your fingertips, then stir in the sugar followed by a pinch of salt. Now, using a knife, mix in the milk little by little, and when it's all in, flour your hands and knead the mixture to a soft dough (you may find you need just a drop more milk if it feels at all dry). Place your dough now on a floured pastry board and with a rolling pin (also floured) lightly roll it out to a thickness of about ¾ inch (2 cm). Then take a 1½- or 2-inch (4·5 cm) pastry cutter (fluted or plain, it doesn't matter) and tap it sharply so that it goes straight through the dough—do *not* twist or the scones will turn out a strange shape!

When you have cut as many as you can, knead the dough together again and repeat. Then place the scones on a greased baking tin, dust each one with flour, and bake near the top of the oven for 12–15 minutes. When they're done they will have risen and turned a golden brown—then transfer them to a wire rack and eat as soon as they are cool enough, spread with Devon butter, jam and clotted cream.

Note: These scones are best eaten as fresh as possible, but if you do have any over—which I doubt—warm them in the oven the next day. Also, if you have no pastry-cutter, you can cut them into small triangles with a knife.

Treacle Scones   (About 10 scones)

8 oz plain flour (225 g)
½ teaspoon salt
4 teaspoons baking powder
¼ teaspoon mixed spice
1½ oz soft brown sugar (40 g)
2 oz butter or margarine (50 g)
about ¼ pint milk (150 ml)
2 tablespoons black treacle

Pre-heat the oven to gas mark 7 (425 °F) (220 °C)

A lightly greased baking sheet.

Start by sifting the flour, salt, baking powder and spice into a bowl. Then stir in the sugar and rub in the fat to the crumbly stage. Now pour all but about 2 tablespoons of milk from the measured ¼ pint (150 ml) into a separate bowl and stir in the black treacle. Now pour the milk/treacle liquid into the dry ingredients and mix to a soft, but not sticky, dough; add some of the remaining 2 tablespoons of milk if necessary—but be careful because you may not need it all. Next turn the dough out on to a lightly floured surface and knead briefly. Then roll it out to a round about ½ inch (1 cm) thick and, using a 2¼-inch (6 cm) fluted cutter, cut out the scone rounds. This may seem a rather small sized cutter but these scones tend to spread rather more than usual. Re-roll and cut out any remaining dough. You should get about ten scones in all. Then place them on the lightly greased baking sheet and bake 12–15 minutes.

Rich Fruit Scones

(Makes 12 scones)

These little scones are so quick and easy to make you could probably have them on the table about 25 minutes after you'd first thought about them.

8 oz self-raising flour (225 g)
2 tablespoons caster sugar
2 oz mixed dried fruit (50 g)
3 oz butter or margarine (75 g)
1 large egg, beaten
about 3–4 tablespoons milk to mix

Pre-heat the oven to gas mark 7 (425 °F) (220 °C)

A lightly greased baking sheet.

First put the flour, sugar and fat in a bowl, then rub the fat into the dry ingredients until the mixture looks crumbly. Now sprinkle in the dried fruit, pour in the beaten egg and add 3 tablespoons of milk. Start to mix to a dough—it should be a soft but not a sticky dough, so add more milk (a teaspoon at a time) if the dough seems too dry. Then form the dough into a ball and turn it out on to a lightly floured working-surface. Now roll it out very lightly to an oblong that's about ½ inch (1 cm) thick. Cut into six squares, then cut the squares in half (to make twelve triangles). Put these wedges on the lightly greased baking sheet and dust lightly with flour. Bake the scones in the top half of the oven for 12–15 minutes or until the scones are well risen and golden brown. Remove them to a cooling tray and serve very fresh, split and spread with butter.

Wheatmeal Date Scones

(Makes 8–10 scones)

For wheatmeal scones I seem to get the best results using half wholemeal and half white flour and these are especially good made with chopped dates.

½ teaspoon salt
2 teaspoons baking powder
4 oz plain flour (110 g)
4 oz wholemeal flour (110 g)
1 oz soft brown sugar (25 g)
½ teaspoon cinnamon
1 oz butter (25 g)
2 oz dates, chopped (50 g)
about ¼ pint milk (150 ml)

Pre-heat the oven to gas mark 8 (450 °F) (230 °C)

A lightly greased baking sheet.

Begin by sifting the salt, baking powder and flours together into a bowl. Then mix in the sugar and cinnamon, and rub the butter in. After that stir in the chopped dates. Now, using a fork, stir in just enough milk to form a soft dough—you'll find that you probably won't need the whole ¼ pint (150 ml). Now turn the dough out on to a floured surface and roll it out to about ¾ inch (2 cm) thick, then using a 2¼-inch (6 cm) plain cutter cut out the scone rounds (re-rolling any trimmings). Arrange them on a greased baking sheet then brush the tops with the rest of the milk and bake near the top of the oven for 10–12 minutes. Then cool them on a wire rack, and eat them preferably warm with plenty of creamy butter.

Cheese Crusted Scones

These are lovely eaten warm from the oven in winter after a long chilly walk.

6 oz self-raising flour (175 g)
1 oz butter
3 oz finely grated strong Cheddar cheese (75 g)
1 large egg
2–2½ tablespoons milk
½ teaspoon salt
½ teaspoon mustard powder
a couple good pinches cayenne pepper
and a little extra milk

Pre-heat the oven to gas mark 7 (425 °F) (220 °C)

A well-greased baking sheet.

Start by measuring the flour into a bowl, add the mustard, salt and one really good pinch of cayenne. Then mix them in thoroughly and rub the butter in, using your finger tips, until it's all crumbly. Then mix in nearly all the grated cheese (leaving about 1 tablespoon over). Now beat the egg with 2 tablespoons of milk and add it to the dry ingredients to make a soft dough— if it seems a little dry add another ½ tablespoon of milk or enough to make a soft smooth dough that will leave the bowl clean. Then roll it out as evenly as possible to around ¾ inch (2 cm) thick and, using a 2¼-inch (6 cm) fluted cutter, cut out the scones. In all you should get about eight. Now place them on a well greased baking sheet, brush the tops with milk, then sprinkle the rest of the grated cheese on top of each scone along with a faint sprinkling of cayenne. Bake them on a high shelf for about 15–20 minutes. Then cool a little on a wire tray, but serve warm, spread with lots of butter.

Note: If you have to prepare a lunch box for anyone, these little scones spread with butter are almost as good eaten cold.

Potato Scones

(About 10 scones)

Unlike some other types of scones, potato scones keep beautifully moist for a day or two after baking, so they're good to put in a lunch box when spread with plenty of butter.

6 oz plain white flour (175 g)
½ teaspoon salt
3 level teaspoons baking powder
2 oz butter or margarine (50 g)
1½ oz caster sugar (40 g)
4 oz freshly boiled mashed potato (110 g)
About 4 tablespoons milk, to mix

Pre-heat the oven to gas mark 7 (425 °F) (220 °C)

A lightly greased baking sheet.

First sift the flour, salt and baking powder into a bowl. Then rub in the fat until the mixture becomes crumbly. Stir in the sugar and after that rub in the mashed potato. Add the milk next and mix to a soft, but not sticky, dough. Now turn the dough out on to a lightly floured surface and knead very lightly. Then roll the mixture out to a round about ½ inch (1 cm) thick. Then using a 2¼ inch (6 cm) fluted cutter cut out the scones; re-rolling any trimmings and cutting again. You should get about 10 scones in all. Place them on the lightly greased baking sheet and bake in the top half of the oven for 12–15 minutes, or until well risen and lightly browned on top. These are really nice served warm, split and buttered.

Drop Scones

(Makes about 24)

Drop scones are like very thick pancakes and they should be served warm with butter melting over them—honey or syrup can be spread on too, or you could eat them American-style on warm plates with maple syrup and cream.

8 oz self-raising flour (225 g)
½ pint milk/water (mixed half and half) (275 ml)
1 standard egg
1 rounded tablespoon caster sugar—more if you like
½ teaspoon bicarbonate of soda
1 teaspoon cream of tartar

lard for greasing.

Sift the dry ingredients into a bowl. Make a well in the centre, then break the egg into this and start whisking, gradually adding the milk/water until you have a smooth lump-free batter.

Heat a griddle, girdle or thick-based frypan, and wipe round it with a piece of greased (larded) greaseproof paper. Now pour the mix from the tip of a large tablespoon on to the heated surface (this will ensure you have even, round pancakes). Then cook until golden brown on the underside and tiny holes start appearing on top. Flip the pancakes over and carry on cooking. As they come off the griddle keep the pancakes covered on a plate lined with a cloth napkin, and serve as soon as possible.

Meringues

(Makes 16)

As with the Pavlova on page 197, with meringues it's all really a question of drying them out rather than attempting to cook them quickly. Provided you beat the egg whites properly, you should never have any trouble.

3 large, fresh egg whites
6 oz caster sugar (175 g)
¼ pt double cream, whipped (150 ml)

Pre-heat the oven to gas mark 2 (300 °F) (150 °C)

Begin by preparing a large baking sheet, oiling it lightly then lining it with greaseproof paper which should also be oiled, or even better than that, line it with some non-stick Bakewell paper.

Now, place the egg whites in a very large, clean, grease-free bowl. Whisk them until they form stiff peaks. Then whisk in the sugar, 1 oz at a time, whisking well after each addition, (I find an electric hand whisk very useful for this). Now take 2 dessertspoons, and spoon sixteen meringues on to the lined baking sheet, using one dessertspoon to spoon the mixture and the other to help form the shape.

Now place them in the oven, then immediately turn the heat down to gas mark 1 (275 °F) (140 °C), and leave them to cook for 1 hour. Then turn the heat right out but *leave* the meringues in the oven to dry out until it's completely cold. A good idea is to leave them overnight. To serve, sandwich the meringues together with whipped cream.

Biscuits

Commercially made biscuits have now become atrociously expensive, and the packaging gets more and more devious. You can so easily pick up what looks like a $\frac{1}{2}$ lb packet but which turns out to be only 6 oz! At the time of writing 12 oz of ginger nuts cost 23p to buy, while homemade the same quantity cost a mere 9½p. Similarly digestives, which cost 21p for 12 oz in the shops, work out at 12½p to make yourself.

The fact is, with biscuit-making the time involved is negligible, as they're so easy to mix and quick to bake: both the ginger nuts and the ginger oat biscuits in this chapter don't even require rolling out—the mixture goes straight on to the baking trays. Another saving is to make your own biscuits for serving with cheese (most impressive at a dinner-party!) or little cheese-flavoured biscuits which, cut out really small, make interesting nibbles with drinks before a meal. Oh, and one thing I nearly forgot to mention—and that's how much better homemade biscuits taste.

Shortbreads

These are my favourite shortbread biscuits, made with fine semolina which gives a lovely light crunchy texture.

6 oz plain flour (175 g)
3 oz caster sugar (85 g)
6 oz butter (room temperature) (175 g)
3 oz fine semolina (85 g)

Pre-heat the oven to gas mark 2 (300 °F) (150 °C)

You'll need an oblong tin measuring 11 × 7 inches (28 × 18 cm) lightly greased.

Warm a mixing bowl slightly—it mustn't be hot, just warm —then add all the ingredients and beat with a wooden spoon till thoroughly blended (because of the high fat content there's no need to add any liquid). Now transfer the dough on to a lightly sugared flat surface. Roll it out to a rectangle to fit into the tin. Press it out evenly then prick it all over with a fork and bake slowly for 1 hour. Then cool for 10 minutes; cut the mixture into fingers and cool them on a wire rack before storing in a tin.

Sesame Biscuits   (Makes about 50)

These are very crisp and crunchy with the delicious flavour of toasted sesame seeds.

5 oz sesame seeds (150 g) (available at wholefood shops)
9 oz light soft brown sugar (250 g)
6 oz butter or margarine, melted (175 g)
1 standard egg, beaten
1 teaspoon vanilla essence
6 oz plain flour (175 g)
¼ teaspoon baking powder
¼ teaspoon salt

Pre-heat the oven to gas mark 5 (375 °F) (190 °C)

Some well-greased baking sheets.

First spread the sesame seeds on a dry baking sheet and bake in the pre-heating oven for about 5–8 minutes or until they're roasted to a good beigy-brown colour. Then remove from the oven and let them cool. Meanwhile sieve the brown sugar into a bowl (to extract any lumps). Then stir in the melted fat, beaten egg and vanilla essence, followed by the sesame seeds, flour, baking powder and salt. Stir till thoroughly mixed. Now drop half-teaspoons of the mixture on to well greased baking sheets, allowing the mixture room to spread during baking. Then bake them in the centre of the oven for 10 minutes. The biscuits will go a slightly dark brown colour and look lacey around the edges. When they're cooked remove the baking sheets and leave the biscuits to cool for 3 minutes before removing with a thin palette knife to a wire rack. As soon as they are cool store them in an airtight container to keep them really crisp.

Ginger Oat Biscuits (Makes 18)

These are very simple to make and, like the gingernuts, they don't have to be rolled or cut out, in fact you could make them from start to finish in about 25 minutes flat.

4 oz butter or margarine (110 g)
1 dessertspoon golden syrup
3 oz demerara sugar (75 g)
4 oz self-raising flour (110 g)
4 oz whole Jumbo oats (or porridge oats) (110 g)
1 rounded teaspoon ground ginger
pinch of salt

Pre-heat the oven to gas mark 3 (325 °F) (170 °C)

Two baking sheets lightly greased.

First, gently heat the margarine, sugar and syrup together in a small saucepan until the fat has dissolved. Meanwhile sift the flour into a bowl, then stir in the oats, ginger and salt. Now pour the melted mixture in and mix very thoroughly. Then take smallish blobs of the mixture (a bit more than a heaped teaspoonful) roll them into little balls with your hand and place about 9 of these on each baking sheet. Space them well so that they have room to expand, which they do quite a bit. Press each one to flatten a little bit, then bake them for about 10–15 minutes, or until they've turned a lovely golden brown colour. Leave them on the baking sheet for 15 minutes, then transfer them to a wire rack to finish cooling. Store them in an airtight tin to keep really crisp.

Shrewsbury Biscuits

(Makes about 36 thin biscuits or 20 thicker ones)

You can flavour these biscuits with either caraway seeds or currants—whichever you prefer.

8 oz plain flour (225 g)
4 oz butter or margarine (110 g)
4 oz caster sugar (110 g)
2 teaspoons caraway seeds, or 2 oz currents (50 g)
1 standard egg, beaten
1 teaspoon water
a little additional caster sugar

Pre-heat the oven to gas mark 4 (350 °F 180 °C)

You'll need lightly greased baking sheets.

Begin by putting the flour, sugar and fat in a bowl. Then rub in the fat until the mixture resembles fine breadcrumbs. Then sprinkle in the caraway seeds (or currants), pour in the beaten egg and water and mix to a firm dough. Now turn it out on to a lightly floured surface and roll out to about $\frac{1}{8}$ inch (3 mm) thick. If you've added currants, make it thicker—about $\frac{1}{4}$ inch ($\frac{1}{2}$ cm). Then cut out the biscuit rounds, using a 2$\frac{3}{4}$-inch (7 cm) fluted cutter and lay the biscuits on the lightly greased baking sheets. Then sprinkle lightly with additional caster sugar and bake for about 15 minutes or until the biscuits feel firm and have turned a pale golden colour. Leave them to cool on the baking sheets for a few minutes before removing them to a wire rack to finish cooling. Store in an airtight container.

Jean's Gingernuts

It was at my friend Jean's house that I first tasted these really light, crunchy gingernut biscuits and, luckily, she gave me the recipe.

4 oz self-raising flour (110 g)
1 slightly rounded teaspoon ground ginger
1 level teaspoon bicarbonate of soda
1½ oz granulated sugar (40 g)
2 oz margarine (50 g)
2 oz (or 2 tablespoons) golden syrup (50 g)

Pre-heat the oven to gas mark 5 (375 °F) (190 °C)

One large or two small baking sheets lightly greased.

Sift the flour, ground ginger and bicarbonate of soda together into a mixing bowl, add the sugar then lightly rub in the margarine till crumbly. All you do now is, simply, add the syrup and mix everything to a stiff paste. No liquid is needed because the syrup will be enough to bring the mixture to the right consistency. Now divide the mixture into sixteen pieces, as even sized as possible, and roll the pieces into little balls. Then place them on the baking sheet, leaving plenty of room between them because they spread out quite a bit. Then just flatten them slightly and bake a little above the centre of the oven for 15–20 minutes by which time they will have spread themselves out and will have a lovely cracked appearance. Cool them on the baking tray for 10 minutes or so, then transfer them to a wire rack to finish cooling and store in an airtight tin.

Oat and Raisin Crunchies (Makes about 30)

I am always amazed at how easy it is to make biscuits, and with this recipe there isn't even any rubbing in, rolling or cutting out to do.

3 oz butter or margarine (75 g)
6 oz soft brown sugar, sieved (175 g)
7 oz medium oatmeal (200 g)
4 oz wholewheat flour (110 g)
½ teaspoon bicarbonate of soda
½ teaspoon salt
3 oz raisins (75 g)
1 standard egg, beaten

Pre-heat the oven to gas mark 4 (350 °F) (180 °C)

Greased baking sheets.

Begin by heating the fat in a small saucepan very gently then, when it's melted, remove it from the heat and leave it to cool a little before stirring in the beaten egg. Now measure the rest of the ingredients into a bowl, then pour in the egg/fat mixture and stir to a stiff paste. Form the paste into little balls, about the size of a walnut, and place them on greased baking sheets, giving them enough room to spread slightly during the baking. Bake for about 10 to 12 minutes by which time the biscuits should feel fairly firm in the centre. Leave them to cool on the baking sheets. Then ease them off using a palette knife and store in an airtight tin.

Macaroons

(Makes 3 dozen)

These crisp little almond biscuits are a speciality of the Lorraine region in France. They're easy to make and are particularly nice served with fruit fools or ice-cream.

6 oz ground almonds (175 g)
1 oz icing sugar (25 g)
1 teaspoon ground rice
8 oz granulated sugar (225 g)
3 standard egg whites
a few drops of almond essence
some caster sugar
about 12 blanched almonds cut into strips
some rice paper

Pre-heat the oven to gas mark 2 (300 °F) (150 °C)

First line two large baking sheets with rice paper. If you can't get hold of rice paper, line the baking sheets with non-stick Bakewell paper (from W. H. Smith's) or, failing that, oil the baking sheets and line them with greaseproof paper also oiled with a flavourless oil (groundnut oil).

In a bowl mix the ground almonds together with the sifted icing sugar, ground rice and granulated sugar. Now stir in the unbeaten egg whites and a few drops of almond essence and continue stirring until very thoroughly mixed. Place the mixture in a forcing bag fitted with a ¾-inch (2 cm) plain nozzle and pipe out rounds of the mixture on to the rice paper, allowing room between each for the biscuits to expand during cooking. Then sprinkle each one with caster sugar and top it with a piece of blanched almond. Now bake the biscuits for about 25–30 minutes, or until they are tinged a light golden brown. Leave them to cool then strip off the rice paper surrounding each biscuit (or remove them from the paper). Store them in an airtight tin as soon as they have cooled if you like to eat them crisp or, if you prefer them a bit chewy, leave them overnight before storing in a tin.

Almond Tuiles

These are deliciously light little biscuits to serve with fruit fools, purées or ice-cream—or just to eat on their own!

2 egg whites
4 oz caster sugar (110 g)
2 oz plain flour (50 g)
a few drops each of vanilla and pure almond essence
2 oz flaked almonds (50 g)
2 oz butter, melted (50 g)

Pre-heat the oven to gas mark 7 (425 °F) (220 °C)

First butter two baking sheets and dust them with flour.

Then place the egg whites in a very clean bowl and whisk until stiff but not dry. Now beat in the sugar bit by bit and continue beating until the mixture forms soft peaks. When that happens carefully fold in the rest of the ingredients. Next take about half a teaspoon of the mixture at a time, dropping them on to a baking sheet—spacing them very wide apart—(though you'll only be able to get two or three blobs on each baking sheet at a time because you need to spread them out so). Using forks, tease out each blob into a thin lacey disc about 1½ inches (4 cm) in diameter, and don't worry about a small hole here and there—it doesn't matter at all. Now bake the biscuits in the centre of the oven for 5–8 minutes or until the biscuits have turned a nice golden colour with a fine brown fringe. Remove each disc carefully from the baking sheet, using a metal spatula, then curve each biscuit immediately over a rolling-pin, and leave a few minutes until each biscuit is cool and crisp. Then remove them to a wire rack, and continue in this way until all the mixture has been used up. Store the biscuits immediately in an airtight tin to keep them crisp.

Soda Biscuits

8 oz plain flour (225 g)
4 oz caster sugar (110 g)
2 oz butter or margarine (50 g)
1 standard egg, beaten
¾ teaspoon bicarbonate of soda
milk

Pre-heat the oven to gas mark 4 (350 °F) (180 °C)

First combine the flour and sugar together in a mixing bowl. Then rub the fat into the dry ingredients until the mixture resembles fine breadcrumbs. Now make a well in the centre and pour in the beaten egg. Then in a cup dissolve the bicarbonate of soda in 2 teaspoons of water, stir and pour this in with the egg. Mix to a stiff, pliable paste. It may need just a little more liquid so use one or two teaspoons more—of milk, to give the right consistency. Now roll the paste out on a lightly floured surface to about ⅛ inch (3 mm) thick. Cut it into rounds using a 2¼-inch (6 cm) floured, fluted cutter. Bake the biscuits on a greased baking sheet for 12–15 minutes, or until the biscuits have turned a nice golden colour and feel firm when pressed lightly in the centre with a fingertip. Allow them to cool a little before removing with a palette knife to a wire rack to cool.

Chocolate Orange Biscuits

These are rather addictive so it's best to ration them or they'll disappear too quickly.

2 oz margarine (50 g)
3 oz lard (75 g)
6 oz caster sugar (175 g)
8 oz plain flour (225 g)
2 teaspoons baking powder
3 oz plain chocolate, chopped (75 g)

the grated rind of 2 oranges
about 1 tablespoon orange juice

To decorate: extra caster sugar

Pre-heat the oven to gas mark 4 (350 °F) (180 °C)

Start by beating the fats and sugar together until they're pale
and fluffy, then sift the flour and baking powder straight on to
the creamed mixture. Add the rest of the ingredients, and work
the mixture together until you get a fairly stiff paste. Now
flour a working surface and a rolling pin and roll the paste out
to between ¼ and ½ inch thick, (½–1 cm) then using a 2-inch
(5 cm) plain cutter, cut out the biscuits and place them on
greased baking sheets. Sprinkle the biscuits with a little
additional caster sugar, then bake them for about 20 minutes,
or until the biscuits are a nice golden colour. Take them out of
the oven and leave them to cool on the baking sheets for 5 minutes, then cool on a wire rack, and store in an airtight tin.

Langue de Chat Biscuits

The perfect biscuits for serving with sorbets or fruit fools.

2 oz butter (room temperature) (50 g)
2 oz caster sugar (50 g)
2–3 drops vanilla essence
2 standard egg whites
2 oz plain flour, sifted (50 g)
a nylon piping-bag fitted with a ¼-inch (½ cm) plain nozzle

Pre-heat the oven to gas mark 7 (425 °F) (220 °C)

First butter two baking sheets, dust them with a little flour and
tap off any excess flour.

Then cream the butter, sugar and vanilla essence very
thoroughly until the mixture is pale and fluffy. Next put the
egg whites into a bowl—don't whisk them though, just add
them to the mixture a teaspoonful at a time, beating thoroughly

after each addition. When the egg white is all in, lightly fold in the flour then spoon the mixture into the piping bag, then pipe out some 3-inch (7·5 cm) lengths on to the prepared baking sheets. Remember to leave a good space in between each one, because they expand and spread out during the cooking. The mixture should make approximately two dozen. Now bake them on a high shelf in the oven for about 8 minutes, or until they've turned golden and are fringed with brown round the edges. Leave them on the baking sheet for a couple of minutes, then cool them on a wire tray. When cold, store in an airtight tin to keep them nice and crisp.

Wholemeal Oat Biscuits

These are nice just on their own, or with a lump of cheese and a crisp apple for lunch.

4 oz wholemeal flour (110 g)
4 oz medium oatmeal or rolled oats (110 g)
4 oz margarine (110 g)
3 tablespoons demerara sugar
1 egg

Pre-heat the oven to gas mark 5 (375° F) (190 °C)

Lightly grease a baking sheet.

After weighing out all the dry ingredients into a mixing bowl, rub in the margarine. Then beat the egg and add it to the mixture—to bind everything together to a dryish, workable dough. Then transfer the dough on to a very lightly floured surface, and roll it out to a thickness of approximately $\frac{1}{4}$ inch ($\frac{1}{2}$ cm). Now, using a $2\frac{1}{2}$-inch (6·5 cm) pastry cutter, cut the dough into little rounds. Place them on the baking sheet, and bake for 10–15 minutes on a high shelf. Allow them to cool for a minute or two, then transfer them on to a wire tray. When they're cold, store in an airtight tin to keep them crisp.

Digestive Biscuits

These are cheaper to make than buy and much nicer, especially served with some strong cheese and crisp celery.

4 oz wholemeal flour (110 g)
4 oz medium oatmeal (110 g)
½ oz brown sugar (or 1 oz if you like them sweeter) (10–25 g)
3 oz margarine (room temperature) (75 g)
½ teaspoon vinegar
½ teaspoon bicarbonate of soda
a pinch of salt
1 tablespoon milk

Pre-heat the oven to gas mark 4 (350 °F) (180 °C)

Greased baking sheets.

First measure the flour and oatmeal into a bowl, then add the salt, bicarbonate of soda, vinegar and sugar and mix thoroughly. Now rub in the margarine until the mixture is crumbly, then add the milk and mix to a dough. Transfer the dough on to a very lightly floured board to roll out—fairly thin or just under ⅛ inch (3 mm) thick. Cut the biscuits out with a 2½-inch (6·5 cm) cutter, then bake them slightly higher than the centre of the oven for about 15–20 minutes or until just tinged with colour, but be careful not to over-bake. Cool the biscuits on a wire cooling tray and store in an airtight tin.

Little Cheese Biscuits

These are very quick and easy to make, and ideal for serving with drinks at a party or, made slightly bigger, for tucking into a lunch box.

2 oz plain flour (50 g)
2 oz grated Parmesan cheese (50 g)
2 oz butter (room temperature) (50 g)
¼ teaspoon salt
1 pinch cayenne pepper
1 twist ground black pepper
2 oz Cheshire cheese, grated (50 g)

Then for the toppings:
garlic salt
celery salt
mild curry powder
cayenne

Pre-heat the oven to gas mark 5 (375 °F) (190 °C)

Grease a baking sheet.

Then sift the flour into a bowl and add the salt, cayenne and black pepper. Next add the Parmesan cheese and butter and rub the mixture to the crumbly stage. Now, using a fork, stir in the grated Cheshire cheese then, using your hands, bring the mixture together to form a dough. As Cheshire cheese is usually fairly moist you shouldn't need any liquid but, if it seems dry, add just a spot of milk. Then roll the dough out fairly thinly to a thickness of around ⅛ inch (3 mm) and, using a small 1 or 1½-inch (2·5 or 4 cm) cutter, cut the biscuits out and arrange them on the greased baking sheet. They don't spread out during the cooking so you can arrange them fairly close together. Leave them plain if you like or sprinkle them with any of the suggested toppings above. Bake the biscuits for 10–12 minutes on a high shelf then remove them to a cooling rack to cool and crisp. Then store them in a tin.

Biscuits for Cheese

(Makes 24)

These are delicious and it's *so* much nicer to serve homemade biscuits with cheese instead of the packet sort.

6 oz wholewheat flour (175 g)
2 oz porridge oats (50 g)
2 oz lard (50 g)
2 oz butter (50 g)
4 teaspoons soft brown sugar
1 teaspoon baking powder
½ teaspoon salt
¼ teaspoon hot curry powder
about 1 tablespoon milk, to bind

Pre-heat the oven to gas mark 4 (350 °F) (180 °C)

A lightly greased baking sheet.

Just combine all the ingredients together in a bowl, except for the milk. Then rub the fat evenly into the ingredients and add enough milk to make a slightly wetter dough than you would normally for, say, shortcrust pastry. This pastry is prone to breaking, because of the oats, so the little extra moisture helps to hold it together. Now turn it out on to a floured working surface and roll out to about ⅛ inch (3 mm) thick. Use a plain 2¾-inch (7 cm) cutter to cut out the biscuit rounds, then place them on a lightly greased baking sheet—they can be arranged quite close together as they don't spread out much during cooking. Bake them for 15–20 minutes until lightly browned and firm. Then leave them to cool on the baking sheet for 5 minutes before transferring them to a wire rack to cool. Store in a tin.

Note: If, when you re-roll the trimmings, the dough becomes a little dry, add a touch more milk to moisten it.

Homemade Florentines (Makes about 3 dozen)

These very luxurious biscuits can't be dashed off in five minutes but, if you have the time, then they do make a marvellous present to give at Christmas time.

2 tablespoons butter (plus a little extra)
6 oz caster sugar (175 g)
1 oz plain flour (25 g)
½ pint double cream (275 ml)
4 oz whole almonds, blanched and cut into thin slivers (110 g)
4 oz ready-flaked almonds (110 g)
4 oz chopped candied peel (110 g)
2 oz glacé cherries, chopped (50 g)
2 oz angelica, finely chopped (50 g)
approx 8 oz plain chocolate (225 g)

Pre-heat the oven to gas mark 5 (375 °F) (190 °C)

You'll need baking sheets, some greaseproof paper and a 2½-inch (6·5 cm) pastry cutter.

Start by melting 2 tablespoons of butter together with the sugar and flour in a heavy saucepan over a very low heat, then keep stirring until the mixture has melted and is absolutely smooth. Now gradually add the cream (stirring continuously to keep it smooth). Then add all the remaining ingredients, *except* the chocolate. Stir thoroughly again, then remove the saucepan from the heat and put the mixture on one side to cool. Next, brush the baking sheets with melted butter, dust with a little flour and then tap them to get rid of the excess flour. Now place teaspoonfuls of the mixture on the prepared baking sheets, spacing them about an inch apart (to allow the mixture room to expand while baking). Flatten each spoonful with the back of the spoon, then bake on a high shelf for about 10 minutes, or until the edges of the biscuits are beginning to tinge brown. If, at this stage, they look like spreading out too much, use the pastry cutter (well greased) to ease them back into a neat round shape. Then give them another 5 minutes baking, till golden. Leave the biscuits to harden on the baking sheets for 3 minutes, before removing them to a wire rack to cool. Next melt the chocolate in a basin over a saucepan of barely simmering water, then spread the liquid chocolate in a layer roughly ⅛ inch (3 mm) thick, on sheets of greaseproof paper.

Place the cooled Florentines, base-down, on the warm melted chocolate, and leave them until cold and set. Then, using the same cutter, cut out each biscuit complete with its new chocolate base (all the chocolate trimmings can be peeled off the greaseproof paper and melted again). Now, with a knife, spread a little melted chocolate (trimmings) on the new-set chocolate base on each Florentine, and just before it sets make a patterned wavy line on it using a fork. Then leave them to set again. Pack the Florentines in alternating rows of fruit and chocolate side up in boxes or tins.

Pudding Cakes

When is a cake not a cake? When it's a pudding. This half-and-half category has long been a favourite on sweet-trolleys in all manner of restaurants, decorated up to the nines to tempt the flagging palate. Yet so often they fail dismally to live up to their promise. Of course presentation is important, but not if it is simply a disguise for blandness.

A few pudding-cakes have already appeared in this book, especially in the chocolate section, but there are plenty of others that are equally at home served at tea-time or as a sweet course at dinner. It's in this section, for instance, that I have included the famous Pavlova cake—to my mind one of the nicest pudding courses of all when the soft summer fruits are in season.

I'm often getting letters from failed meringue-makers, but once it's explained properly no one need have a moment's anxiety; and as for mastering the way to whip egg whites, follow the directions on page 197 and you shouldn't ever have problems. And if the meringue cracks a little while it's cooking, so what? It doesn't matter a bit, in fact I would suggest a few cracks here and there are a sure sign they are homemade and not the insipidly perfect factory-made version.

It's very easy to get carried away by one's ambitions, yet it frequently turns out the simplest ideas are the most effective. Like Strawberry Shortcake, an excellent summer pudding: simply a base of crisp shortbread covered with whipped cream and piled high with strawberries, but what could be more delicious?

Apricot Hazelnut Meringue Cake (Serves 6)

This is a very light, soft meringue mixture—not over-crisp on the outside and fairly 'marsh-mallowey' on the inside.

3 large egg whites
6 oz caster sugar (175 g)
3 oz ground hazelnuts (75 g)
½ pint double cream (275 ml)
a few whole toasted hazelnuts

Then for the filling:
4 oz dried apricots (110 g) (soaked overnight)
the juice of a small orange
a small strip of orange peel
½-inch (1 cm) cinnamon stick
2 teaspoons arrowroot
1 tablespoon brown sugar

Pre-heat the oven to gas mark 5 (375 °F) (190 °C)

Begin by preparing the tins and you'll need two 7-inch (18 cm) sandwich tins, lightly oiled with a tasteless oil and the bases lined, preferably with silicone (Bakewell) paper or, failing that, greaseproof paper also lightly oiled.

In a large bowl whisk the egg whites to the stiff peak stage. Then whisk in the sugar—roughly an ounce at a time—then take a metal spoon and lightly and gently fold in the ground hazelnuts. Now divide the mixture into the prepared tins and spread it out as evenly as possible. Bake the meringues on the centre shelf of the oven for about 20–40 minutes. Remove them from the oven and let them cool in the tins for about half an hour before turning out. Don't worry if the surface of the meringue looks uneven, as this is quite normal with a meringue mixture.

When they've cooled loosen them round the edges and turn them out on to a wire rack, then strip off the base papers. To prepare the filling, drain the soaked apricots in a sieve fitted over a bowl. Then place the drained apricots in a small saucepan along with the orange juice, peel, cinnamon, sugar and 2 tablespoons of their soaking water and simmer gently, with a lid on, for about 10–15 minutes. Now mix the 2 teaspoons of arrowroot with a little cold water, add this to the apricot mixture and stir—still keeping the heat fairly low—until the mixture has thickened. Then remove it from the heat and let it get absolutely cold.

About 2 hours before you want to serve the cake, whip the cream, then carefully spread the cooled apricot mixture over one half of the meringue, followed by half the whipped cream. Then, carefully, position the other half of the meringue on top. Spread the remaining whipped cream on top and decorate round the edges with whole toasted hazelnuts.

Note: Ground hazelnuts are available at wholefood shops and delicatessens.

Strawberry Shortcake (Serves 6)

This is a delicious way to serve strawberries at a summer dinner party or for a special tea, and so easy and trouble-free to make.

For the shortcake:
6 oz plain flour (175 g)
6 oz butter (room temperature) (175 g)
3 oz caster sugar (75 g)
3 oz semolina (75 g)

Then to serve:
½ pint double cream, whipped till stiff (275 ml)
¾ lb hulled strawberries (350 g)
1 teaspoon icing sugar

Pre-heat the oven to gas mark 2 (300 °F) (150 °C)

Lightly grease an 8-inch (20 cm) fluted flan tin with a loose base.

Just measure all the shortcake ingredients into a mixing

bowl, and using your hands work the mixture together to form a dough. No liquid is needed in this—as you work the heat from your hands will mould the ingredients together in about 3 or 4 minutes. Now transfer the dough to a flat surface and roll the paste out to a round approximately 8 inches (20 cm) in diameter. You can achieve this by giving the dough quarter turns as you roll it. Next transfer it to the greased flan tin, then using your hands press it out evenly all over and round the edges. If the surface looks a bit uneven, use a small glass tumbler and roll it lightly to smooth it out. Now you *must* prick the shortbread in several places with a fork. If you don't do this it will start to rise up in the oven. Bake the shortbread for 45–55 minutes on the centre shelf. Let it cool in the tin, then carefully take it out and store it in an airtight tin to keep crisp. Just before serving spread the whipped cream over, top with strawberries and lightly dust with icing sugar.

Little Strawberry Shortcakes (Makes 16)

These are delicious served for a very special tea or as a sweet course at a dinner party—but they don't keep very well so must be eaten on the same day as they're made.

For the shortbread mixture:
4 oz plain flour (110 g)
2 oz caster sugar (50 g)
2 oz fine semolina (50 g)
4 oz butter (110 g) (room temperature)

For the filling and topping:
6 oz full fat cream cheese (175 g) (room temperature)
approx 1¼ lbs (550 g) fresh strawberries, hulled and wiped
6 tablesppons red currant jelly
about 1½ tablespoons orange juice

Pre-heat the oven to gas mark 2 (300 °F) (150 °C)

187

Lightly greased patty tins.

To make the shortcake tartlets, simply combine all the ingredients to form a dough. Because of the high fat content no liquid is needed—you just 'work' the whole lot together. Place the dough in a polythene bag and let it rest in the refrigerator for about 20 minutes. Then roll it out on a floured working surface to just under a $\frac{1}{4}$ inch (0·5 cm) thick. Now, using a fluted $3\frac{1}{4}$-inch (8 cm) cutter, cut out the rounds and carefully ease them into lightly greased patty tins. Prick each one thoroughly all round the base and sides and bake them on the centre shelf of the oven for about 35 minutes, or until they're firm and golden. Then transfer them to a wire rack and leave to cool.

About an hour before serving them, soften the cream cheese a little by beating it with a wooden spoon, then spoon a little into each little tartlet case, pressing it gently all over with your little finger. Now place the larger strawberries in the centre of each tartlet; cut the smaller ones in half and lay these around.

Just before serving, put the red currant jelly and orange juice into a small saucepan over a gentle heat and mash up the jelly with a fork to dissolve it. Then press it through a sieve into a bowl and, when it's almost cool, spoon, or brush, it over the strawberry filling.

Note: A more simple version of this would be to leave out the glaze and merely dust the strawberries with a little bit of caster sugar just before they go to the table.

Peach Pudding Cake

When the fresh peaches start really to come down in price towards the end of August this half-cake, half-pudding, recipe is a nice way to use them.

4 oz plain flour (110 g)
2 oz caster sugar (50 g)

1 teaspoon baking powder
a generous pinch of salt
2 oz butter (50 g)
1 egg
3 tablespoons milk
3 peaches, skinned

And for the topping:
2 oz demerara sugar (50 g)
$\frac{1}{2}$ teaspoon ground cinnamon
$\frac{1}{4}$ teaspoon grated nutmeg
2 tablespoons melted butter

Pre-heat the oven to gas mark 6 (400 °F) (200 °C)

Butter an 8-inch (20 cm) round sandwich tin, at least 1 inch (2·5 cm) deep, then place the flour, sugar, baking powder and salt into a bowl.

Now rub in the butter, until the mixture resembles fine breadcrumbs. Break the egg into a separate basin and beat it together with the milk. Then pour this on to the rubbed-in mixture and stir with a wooden spoon until it forms a soft dough. Next turn the mixture into the prepared tin and carefully level it off with the back of a spoon. Now skin the peaches by placing them in a bowl and pouring over enough boiling water to just cover them. Leave the peaches for a minute or two, then drain and carefully peel off the skins. Slice each peach fairly thinly, discarding the stone and arrange the peach slices over the top of the cake mixture in the tin. In another bowl mix the sugar, cinnamon and nutmeg together and sprinkle this over the top of the peaches. Follow this with a sprinkling of melted butter, then bake for 30–35 minutes or until the mixture is slightly risen and seems lightly browned and bubbly. This is nicest served warm with some very cold pouring cream.

Brandy Snaps

(Makes 18)

All you need to make perfect, crunchy, toffee-tasting brandy snaps is a bit of practice. Once you get the knack, they're very easy and keep well stored in an airtight tin.

2 oz golden syrup (50 g)
1½ oz caster sugar (40 g)
2 oz butter (50 g)
1½ oz plain flour (40 g)
¾ teaspoon ground ginger
1 teaspoon brandy

Pre-heat the oven to gas mark 4 (350 °F) (180 °C)

First grease two baking sheets with butter.

In a thick-based saucepan melt the syrup with the sugar and butter, and heat very gently until the sugar has dissolved and the mixture is smooth. Then remove the saucepan from the heat and beat in the sifted flour and ground ginger, followed by the brandy. Now take teaspoonfuls of the mixture and drop them on to the greased baking sheets, spacing the blobs about 3 inches apart, then bake them in the centre of the oven for about 10 minutes, or until each teaspoonful of mixture has spread to a thin, golden lacy-looking disc. Remove the baking sheets from the oven and then leave the mixture for about 2 minutes before removing the snaps from the sheets with a palette knife. Now roll each one around the handle of a wooden spoon then remove it and leave them all to cool on a wire tray. Repeat all this until the mixture has been used up. (If you get called away in the middle of all this and any cooked mixture cools and becomes too stiff either to remove from the baking sheet or—to roll up easily—place it back in the oven for 2 minutes then try again.) The brandy snaps should only be filled with whipped cream just before serving.

Amaretti Chocolate Cake   (Serves 8)

This is really much more pudding than cake and very rich.
Amaretti biscuits are available at delicatessens and specialised
food shops—they're flavoured with almonds and wrapped in
paper like sweets.

1½ lb box Amaretti biscuits (700 g)
6 oz plain chocolate (175 g)
4 tablespoons brandy
3 tablespoons cider
¾ pint double cream (425 ml)

For the decoration:
grated chocolate
whipped cream

You'll need a lightly oiled 1¾-pint (1 litre) pudding basin.
Then to start break up the chocolate into another basin fitted
over a pan of barely simmering water and leave until melted.
    While that's happening, pour the cream into a saucepan and
heat to just below boiling point, then pour it on to the melted
chocolate and whisk, with an electric mixer, until you have a
cold, creamy chocolate mixture. Next mix the brandy and cider
together, and then dip the biscuits one at a time first into the
liquor then into the chocolate cream, and arrange about 4 or
5 in the base of the pudding basin. Now spread a layer of
chocolate mixture over the first layer of biscuits, then repeat
the whole process until you have four layers. Place a saucer
(one that fits inside the rim of the basin) on top of the mixture,
put a 2- or 3-lb (900 g or 1 kg 350 g) weight on top and leave
in the refrigerator overnight. (Before serving, dip the basin in
hot water for about 3 seconds, turn the pudding out on to a
serving dish, allow the outside to get firm again, then decorate
with blobs of whipped cream and grated chocolate.)

Strawberry and Orange Gâteau

This is good for a June birthday tea—served in the garden if the weather permits.

For cake:
6 oz butter (room temperature) (175 g)
6 oz caster sugar (175 g)
the grated rind of 2 oranges
3 eggs, beaten
1½ tablespoons orange juice
8 oz self-raising flour (225 g)

For the filling:
4 tablespoons orange curaçao (this can be bought in miniature bottles)
¾ lb strawberries (350 g)
1 tablespoon icing sugar
½ pint double cream (275 ml)
¼ pint single cream (150 ml)
1 tablespoon caster sugar

Pre-heat the oven to gas mark 3 (325 °F) (170 °C)

Lightly grease a deep 8-inch (20 cm) round cake tin, and line the base with a circle of greaseproof paper (and lightly grease the paper too).

Next beat the sugar, butter and orange rinds together until the mixture looks light and fluffy. Then gradually add the beaten eggs a little at a time, beating the mixture well between each addition. Now, lightly and carefully, using a metal spoon fold in the orange juice, followed by the flour. The mixture should have a soft dropping consistency—if not, add a little more orange juice. Spread the mixture evenly into the prepared tin, and bake with the top of the tin level with the centre of the oven. It should take about 1¼–1½ hours by which time it will have shrunk away from the sides of the tin and feel springy in the centre. Turn out and leave the cake to cool on a wire rack. When it's cool, cut it carefully with a sharp knife into three rounds. Then sprinkle a little liqueur (say, 2 tablespoons) on the cake rounds. Now hull and wipe the straw-berries, then put aside eight good, even-sized ones for decoration. Quarter the rest and put them in a bowl, sprinkle with icing sugar and pour over 2 tablespoons of curaçao. Then leave them covered in a cool place to soak up the liqueur. To assemble the cake, drain the soaking strawberries and pour the juices into a bowl with the creams. Add a tablespoon of caster sugar and whisk until the cream has thickened. Now put a third of the cream on to the bottom layer and spread evenly with a palette knife and spoon on half the soaked, drained, strawberries. Then press the next round of cake in position, and repeat. Put the top round on, finish off with the rest of the cream and the reserved strawberries, and keep in a cool place—preferably covered—till ready to serve.

Note: It's better to assemble the cake at least 3 or 4 hours before serving, so the cream can weld it together and make it easier to slice.

Cheat's Lemon Gâteau   (Serves 6–8 people)

I love this recipe. There's no cooking involved, it's incredibly easy and, when you serve it, everyone is bound to think you've been slaving away all day! It's also best made the night before or even 3 or 4 days ahead, if you prefer.

8 trifle sponges (from a packet)
4 oz unsalted butter (room temperature) (110 g)
6 oz caster sugar (175 g)
4 eggs, separated
2 large lemons
½ pint double cream (275 ml)

I make this in a 2-pint (approx 1 litre) soufflé dish but, failing that, a 2-pint pudding basin will do.

Start by creaming the butter and sugar till very pale and fluffy. Then in a basin or cup mix the egg yolks together, then beat them into the creamed mixture a little at a time, preferably with an electric hand-whisk. Now grate the lemons and add the grated rinds to the creamed mixture followed by the juice. Next, using a clean bowl and whisk, whisk the egg whites till they stand up in soft peaks. Then, using a large metal spoon, carefully and gently fold them into the creamed mixture. If the mixture shows signs of curdling, ignore it as it doesn't really matter.

To assemble the cake, first split the sponges in half lengthways, then place a layer of them in the base of the bowl, followed by a layer of the mixture and carry on like this finishing off with a layer of sponge. Cover the dish with foil, put a plate on top, then leave it in the refrigerator overnight. To serve, loosen the cake round the edges with a palette knife, turn it out on to a serving plate and serve either cut into slices with pouring cream served separately or alternatively, you can cover it with whipped cream and decorate with lemon slices or more grated lemon.

Orange and Lemon Refrigerator Cake
(Serves 6)

This is a lovely light refreshing sweet course—just the thing to serve after a rich meal, but try to make it the night before.

1 oz butter (melted) (25 g)
6 digestive biscuits, crushed to crumbs
2 tablespoons soft brown sugar
3 large eggs, separated
the finely grated rind and juice of 1 large lemon
the finely grated rind and juice of a smallish orange
2½ oz caster sugar (60 g)
1 tablespoon powdered gelatine
¼ pint double cream (150 ml)

One 2¾-pint (23 × 13 × 6·5 cm) loaf tin, brushed lightly with a tasteless oil like groundnut oil.

In a small basin combine the biscuit crumbs with the brown sugar, then pour in the melted butter and mix thoroughly. Sprinkle a third of this mixture over the base of the loaf tin. Now put the egg yolks, grated rinds and strained orange and lemon juice into a bowl, add the sugar and gelatine too. Then place the bowl over a pan of barely simmering water and whisk for about 10 minutes until the mixture thickens. Then remove the bowl from the heat and whisk again until the mixture cools (an electric hand whisk will be very useful here). Now clean the whisk thoroughly and first beat the egg whites till stiff, then beat the cream until floppy but not too thick. Next take a metal spoon and carefully fold the egg whites first and then the cream into the orange and lemon mixture. Now pour it into the tin, sprinkle the remaining crumbs over the top, cover with foil and transfer it to the freezing compartment of the refrigerator and freeze overnight. An hour before serving transfer the tin to the main body of the refrigerator, then turn it out on to a serving dish and serve cut in slices. If you have any left over, there is no need to re-freeze it; just leave it in the refrigerator where it will become more like a mousse.

Linzertorte

This is a delicious sort of jam lattice tart, made with a lovely hazelnut pastry and named after the town of Linz in Austria.

6 oz plain flour (175 g)
3 oz ground hazelnuts (75 g)
2 oz icing sugar, sifted (50 g)
the finely grated rind of 1 lemon
¼ teaspoon cinnamon
freshly grated nutmeg
4 oz butter (110 g)
2 egg yolks
12 oz jar cranberry jelly (Tiptree do this) (350 g)
2 teaspoons lemon juice

Pre-heat the oven to gas mark 5 (375 °F) (190 °C)

A 9-inch (23 cm) round, fluted flan tin with a removable base, well buttered.

First combine the flour, ground hazelnuts, icing sugar, lemon rind, cinnamon and a few gratings of whole nutmeg in a bowl, then rub in the butter until the mixture is crumbly. Stir in the 2 egg yolks and form the mixture into a dough. Weigh a 5-oz (150 g) piece of the pastry dough and put it to one side, rolling out the rest on a floured surface to a 10-inch (25·5 cm) round. Place this in the base of the tin and, using your fingers, gradually ease the dough up the side of the tin so that it stands up above the edge, then smooth the base out with your hands. Next, mix the jelly with the lemon juice and spoon all but 2 tablespoons on to the pastry, smoothing it out evenly to the edge. Now use the rest of the dough to make a lattice-work pattern on the top, with strips about one-third of an inch (½–1 cm) wide. Then go round the pastry edge with a fork, turning it over inside the edge of the tin to give about a ½-inch (1 cm) border all round. Bake on a high shelf for 30 minutes, or until the pastry is golden brown. Then use the reserved jam to fill up the squares formed by the lattice, as soon as the tart comes out of the oven. Sift icing sugar over the tart and serve it warm or cold with whipped cream.

Pavlova Cake with Summer Fruits

(Serves 6)

With meringues it's a question of once you know how you never look back. If you follow this recipe you should never have a failure provided you beat the egg whites properly in a clean, grease-free bowl and are very careful not to let in any of the yolk.

3 large fresh egg whites
6 oz caster sugar (175 g)
1 level teaspoon cornflour
½ teaspoon vinegar
½ pint whipped cream (275 ml)
¾ lb soft fruits (raspberries, strawberries and redcurrants mixed (350 g)
a little icing sugar

Pre-heat the oven to gas mark 2 (300 °F) (150 °C)

First prepare a baking sheet by oiling it lightly, then line it with greaseproof paper (which should also be oiled lightly).

Place the egg whites in a large clean bowl and have the sugar measured and ready. Now whisk the egg whites until they form soft peaks and you can turn the bowl upside down without them sliding out (it's very important, though, not to over-beat the eggs because, if you do, they will start to collapse).

When they're ready, start to whisk the sugar in approximately 1 oz (25 g) at a time, whisking after each addition and, when all the sugar is in, whisk in the vinegar and cornflour. Now take a metal tablespoon and spoon the meringue mixture on to the prepared baking sheet, forming a circle of about eight inches in diameter. Make a round depression in the centre then, using the tip of a skewer, make little swirls in the meringue all round, lifting the skewer up sharply each time to leave tiny peaks. Now place the baking sheet in the oven, then immediately turn the heat down to gas mark 1 (275 °F) (140 °C) and leave it to cook for one hour. Then turn the heat right out but *leave* the Pavlova inside the oven until it's completely cold—I always find it's best to make a Pavlova in the evening and leave it in the turned-off oven overnight to dry out. It's my belief that the secret of successful meringues of any sort is to let them dry out completely, which is what this method does perfectly.

To serve the Pavlova, lift it from the baking sheet, peel off the paper and place it on a serving dish. Then just before serving, spread the whipped cream on top, arrange the raspberries etc on top of the cream and dust with a little sifted icing sugar. Serve cut into wedges. In the winter, when there are no soft fruits available, sliced bananas and chopped preserved ginger make a nice filling.

Moist Chocolate Hazelnut Gâteau

(Serves 10)

Be warned, this is wickedly rich, a chewy, chocolatey, nutty mixture sandwiched together with whipped cream.

2 oz unsweetened baker's chocolate (50 g)
4 oz butter (110 g)
2 eggs, beaten
8 oz granulated sugar (225 g)
2 oz plain flour (50 g)
1 level teaspoon baking powder
¼ teaspoon salt
4 oz chopped, toasted hazelnuts (or other nuts, walnuts, brazils, almonds etc) (110 g)

To decorate:
½ pint whipped cream (275 ml)
Extra chopped nuts

Pre-heat the oven to gas mark 4 (350 °F) (180 °C)

Grease and line an oblong baking tin 7 × 11 inches (18 × 28 cm) making sure the lining paper stands up at least an inch above the edge of the tin.

Place the butter and chocolate together in a large mixing

bowl fitted over a saucepan of barely simmering water, and allow the chocolate to melt. Then beat it till smooth, remove it from the heat and simply stir in all the other ingredients till thoroughly blended. Now spread the mixture evenly into the prepared tin and bake on the centre shelf for 30 minutes. Leave the cake in the tin for 15 minutes to cool, then remove it from the tin, turn it out on to a cooling tray. Strip off the lining paper and when it's absolutely cold carefully cut the cake in half, down the centre lengthways, so you're left with two oblongs. Now spread half the cream thickly along one half. Position the other half on top, and then spread the rest of the cream all over the cake, covering it completely. Then decorate with chopped nuts or grated chocolate. If all the cake isn't eaten, to keep it fresh store inside a polythene container in the refrigerator.

Note: Instead of cream you could use the chocolate fudge icing on page 87, but that will make it even richer!

Cheesecake

Cheesecakes are not really cakes as such, but lovely creamy concoctions flavoured in a variety of ways, and sometimes covered with delicious toppings. The curious thing is that although cheesecakes pop up all through the history of English cooking, it's in America they have really come into their own, where there are scores of bewildering varieties. Here I have chosen some of the easy-to-make examples, cooked and un-cooked, as well as some Little Cheesecakes which are in fact puffs of pastry with cheese filling, and those delightful and traditional English curd tarts known as Richmond Maids of Honour.

The different types of cream cheese now available can be confusing. Cream cheese isn't technically a cheese but more like concentrated cream: it can be labelled full-fat or medium-fat, but either will do for most recipes. Curd cheese on the other hand *is* a cheese, which has undergone a natural souring process. It has a medium fat content, and gives a lighter texture to a cheese cake than cream cheese. Cottage cheese is simply a low-fat curd cheese, and because its texture is uneven and lumpy it must be sieved or liquidised before being used in a recipe. All the above cheeses are usually available at branches of Sainsbury's.

Cheesecake with Fresh Raspberries

(Serves 10–12)

This is a very large cheesecake, which will go a long way at a party. In the winter you could use slices or chunks of fresh pineapple instead of raspberries.

8 oz wheatmeal biscuits (225 g)
4 oz butter (110 g)
1½ lb curd cheese (700 g)
8 oz sugar (225 g)
3 standard eggs
1 teaspoon vanilla essence

For the topping:
½ pint double cream, whipped (275 ml)
¾ lb fresh raspberries (350 g)
icing sugar

Pre-heat the oven to gas mark 2 (300 °F) (150 °C)

A 9-inch (23 cm) cake tin about 2–3 inches (5–7·5 cm) deep with a loose base.

Gently melt the butter in a small saucepan, without letting it brown. Crush the biscuits to fine crumbs with a rolling pin, then stir them into the melted butter. Transfer the biscuit mixture into the cake tin and press it down evenly all over to form a base. Now combine the curd cheese, eggs and sugar together in a mixing bowl and beat to form a smooth, thick cream—an electric mixer is best for this. Then mix in the vanilla essence and pour the mixture over the biscuit base, smoothing it out evenly.

Cook the cheesecake for 30 minutes on the centre shelf, then turn the oven off and leave it to get quite cold in the oven. It should then be chilled for at least 2 hours, or preferably over-night. To turn the cheesecake out of the tin, rinse a clean dishcloth in hot water. Hold it around the tin for a few seconds, then push up the base very gently.

Just before serving, top the cake with the whipped cream,

arrange the raspberries on top of the cream and dust lightly with icing sugar.

Lemon Cream Cheesecake (Serves 12)

This is a cheesecake for a dinner party or a busy week-end. It's very light and 'moussey' in texture and makes a perfect pudding-like cake.

12 oz curd cheese (or cottage cheese) (350 g)
3½ oz caster sugar (95 g)
grated rind and juice of 3 lemons
1 slightly rounded tablespoon gelatine powder
1 large egg yolk
3 large egg whites
¼ pint single cream (150 ml)
¼ pint double cream (150 ml)
¼ pint milk (150 ml)

Then for the base:
6 digestive biscuits ⎱ crushed to fine crumbs
6 ginger biscuits ⎰
2 oz butter (50 g)

Then for the topping:
4 oz green grapes, peeled, de-pipped and cut in half (110 g)
frosted mint leaves (see note below)

An 8-inch (20 cm) round cake tin with a loose base, lightly oiled with a tasteless groundnut oil.

Begin by making the crumb base. Melt the butter in a small saucepan and mix the crumbs into it. Then press the mixture, as evenly as possible, into the base of the prepared tin.

To make the filling, first place the sugar, milk, grated lemon rinds, gelatine and egg yolk together in a liquidiser. Then whizz them together at top speed for about 30 seconds. Now pour the mixture into a small saucepan and heat it, very gently, stirring all the time. Be careful not to let it come to the boil and, as soon as it feels hot, tip the mixture back into the liquidiser adding the lemon juice and single cream and blend again. While the machine is still running, add the cheese a little at a time until it's all been incorporated and the mixture is absolutely smooth. Then transfer the mixture to a bowl, cover with foil and chill, giving it a stir now and then, until the mixture looks 'syrupy' and is about to set. Now remove it from the refrigerator and whisk it back to a smooth cream. Next, using a clean dry whisk, beat the egg whites to the soft peak stage, then beat the double cream until it just begins to thicken and fold both these into the lemon mixture. Then pour it all into the prepared cake tin, cover with foil again and leave it to chill and set—preferably overnight.

To turn the cheesecake out of the tin, rinse a clean dish-cloth in hot water, then hold it around the tin for a few seconds, then push up the base very gently. To decorate, arrange the peeled grape halves in the centre and around the edge, tucking in a few frosted mint leaves here and there or instead of these you could use very thin lemon slices cut in half.

Note: Frosted mint leaves are made by dipping the leaves first into stiffly beaten egg white, then into caster sugar to get an even coating. Leave them to dry for a couple of hours spread out on greaseproof paper.

Blackcurrant Cheesecake

The tart flavour of blackcurrants goes particularly well with the flavour of cream cheese, and this fairly large cheesecake will serve 8 or 10 people over a busy summer week-end.

1 lb curd cheese (or cottage cheese) (450 g)
4 standard eggs
1 teaspoon vanilla essence
5 oz caster sugar (150 g)
2 teaspoons lemon juice

Then for the base:
8 ginger biscuits
8 digestive biscuits
3 oz butter (75 g)
1 level teaspoon ground cinnamon

Then for the topping:
1 lb blackcurrants, stripped from the stalks (450 g)
3–4 tablespoons caster sugar
2 rounded teaspoons arrowroot

Pre-heat the oven to gas mark 3 (325 °F) (170 °C)

An 8½-inch (21·5 cm) cake tin with a loose base, lightly greased.

Start by placing the cheese, eggs and sugar in a mixing bowl (if you're using cottage cheese, sieve it). Now, using preferably an electric hand-whisk, whisk the mixture together till absolutely smooth. Then add the lemon juice and vanilla essence and mix again thoroughly. Now, melt the butter in a small saucepan; crush the biscuits to fine crumbs and mix them into the butter adding the cinnamon. Mix thoroughly with a fork, then press the biscuit mixture all over the base of the prepared tin as evenly as possible. Now pour the cheese mixture on top of the biscuit base and bake the cheesecake in the centre of the oven for about 30–40 minutes. Then turn the oven out, leave the cheesecake in the warmth of the oven to finish cooking until the oven's cold.

To make the topping, wash the blackcurrants, then place them in a saucepan with the sugar and cook them very gently, without adding any water, until the juice runs out. Then in a small cup mix the arrowroot with a little cold water until smooth then pour this into the blackcurrant mixture and stir gently until the juices have come back to simmering point and the mixture has thickened. Allow this to cool and spread it thickly over the top of the cheesecake after removing it from the tin.

If you like, you can press some more crushed biscuit crumbs round the side of the cheesecake. Then cover with an upturned basin and chill thoroughly before serving.

Quick Lemon Cheesecake   (Serves 6–8)

This is a very quick cheesecake and good to make in hot weather as there's no cooking involved.

For the base:
10 plain digestive biscuits (crushed to crumbs)
2½ oz butter (60 g)
1 teaspoon soft brown sugar

For the filling:
12 oz cottage cheese (350 g)
2½ oz caster sugar (60 g)
the grated rind and juice of 2 lemons
2 large egg yolks
½ oz powdered gelatine (10 g)
¼ pint double cream (150 ml)

You'll also need an 8-inch (20 cm) flan tin or sponge tin with a loose base, lightly oiled.

First prepare the base by melting the butter in a small saucepan, then combining it with the biscuit crumbs and sugar. Spoon the crumb mixture into the prepared tin and press it well down all over as evenly as possible. Now put the gelatine, along with 3 tablespoons cold water, into a small cup and stand this in a small saucepan of barely simmering water. Leave it for about 10 minutes or until the gelatine looks clear and transparent. Then remove it from the heat and leave it on one side.

Now put the egg yolks, sugar and cheese in a liquidiser, blend for about one minute, then add the lemon juice and rind and the gelatine poured through a strainer. Blend again until everything is thoroughly mixed and the mixture absolutely smooth. Next, in a basin, whip the double cream till 'floppy'; add that to the liquidiser and blend again for just a few seconds. Now pour the mixture on to the biscuit base, cover with foil and chill thoroughly for at least 3 hours. Before serving you can, if you wish, add a few thin slices of lemon to decorate.

Rhubarb Cheesecake (Serves 6)

If you can't get hold of curd cheese for this cottage cheese will do but it must be sieved first.

For the crumb base:
5 digestive biscuits, crushed to fine crumbs
5 ginger biscuits crushed to crumbs
2 oz butter, melted (50 g)

For the cheesecake:
12 oz rhubarb, chopped (350 g)
3 oz brown sugar (75 g)
1 level teaspoon ground ginger
3 eggs
6 oz curd cheese (175 g)
2 teaspoons powdered gelatine
¼ pint double cream (150 ml)

One buttered 8-inch (20 cm) cake tin with a removable base.

Place the biscuits in a plastic bag, laying them out flat then, using a rolling pin, crush them to fine crumbs. Mix them with the butter next and press them all over the base of the cake tin. Now put the rhubarb, ginger and sugar in a pan, then cover and cook very gently until soft but not too mushy. In a bowl, beat the eggs, then gradually beat in the cooked rhubarb and juices. Return the mixture to the pan and stir over a low heat until it thickens, but don't allow it to boil or it will curdle. Then remove the pan from the heat, beat in the curd cheese and leave to cool. Now in a small bowl, or old cup, mix the gelatine with 2 tablespoons of water. Leave to soften for a few minutes; then stand the bowl in a pan of hot simmering water and stir until the gelatine liquid is clear; then strain it into the rhubarb mixture. Next, beat the cream to a soft, floppy consistency, then fold it into the rhubarb mixture and pour it into the prepared tin. Cover with foil and chill for several hours before serving.

Little Cheesecakes (Makes about 24)

If you're a bit short of time and elbow grease, I can recommend Sainsbury's puff pastry for these absolutely delectable little cheesecakes, which I'm sure you'll want to make again and again.

10 oz puff pastry (275 g)
4½ oz sugar (125 g)
4½ oz butter or margarine (125 g)
2 large eggs, beaten
3 oz dried plain sponge crumbs (these can be made in a
    liquidiser from trifle sponges) (75 g)
3 oz currants (75 g)
6 oz curd cheese (175 g)
finely grated rind of ½ a small lemon
about ¼ of a nutmeg, freshly grated

Pre-heat the oven to gas mark 6 (400 °F) (200 °C)

First lightly grease some patty tins.

Then on a lightly floured surface roll out the pastry thinly and, using a 3¼-inch (7·5 cm) fluted cutter, cut out small rounds and ease them carefully into the patty tins, pricking the bases well with a fork.

Now cream the fat and sugar together until light and fluffy and beat in the eggs, a little at a time, beating well between each addition. Then stir in all the remaining ingredients. Fill the pastry cases with the mixture and tap the tins on the work surface to settle the mixture evenly. Now bake them for about 25 minutes or until puffy and a fairly deep golden brown. Then leave them to cool in the trays for 5 minutes before removing to a wire rack where they will subside and dip a little in the centre, which they're meant to do—so don't worry.

Strawberry and Orange Cheesecake

This is an uncooked cheesecake, very quick and easy to make and makes a delicious pudding for a summer dinner party.

1½ lb cream cheese (700 g)
4 oz wheatmeal biscuits (110 g)
1 oz butter (25 g)
3 fl oz concentrated frozen orange juice (thawed) (75 ml)
2 oz caster sugar (50 g)
the grated zest of ½ an orange
½ lb strawberries (225 g)

One 8-inch (20 cm) flan tin with a loose base.

First melt the butter, then crush the biscuits to fine crumbs using a rolling-pin. Then in a basin combine them with the melted butter. Now press the biscuit mixture evenly over the base of the flan tin. Next grate the orange zest and blanch it in boiling water for five minutes (to get rid of the bitterness) then leave it to drain thoroughly.

In a large mixing bowl beat the cream cheese, sugar and concentrated orange juice until smooth and free from lumps, then beat in the orange rind. Pour the mixture into the flan tin, spreading it out evenly, cover with foil and chill thoroughly in the refrigerator for several hours. To serve, loosen the base from the side of the tin, and decorate the top of the cake with the strawberries.

Richmond Maids of Honour (Makes about 16)

These little confections are said to be named after the Maids of Honour at Richmond Palace, who created them in the 16th century.

8 oz puff pastry (can be bought frozen, but must be thawed) (225 g)
a little apricot jam
8 oz curd cheese (or cottage cheese sieved) (225 g)
1 larg egg
1 extra yolk
1½ oz caster sugar (40 g)
the grated rind of 1 lemon
1 oz ground almonds (25 g)
1 rounded tablespoon currants

Pre-heat the oven to gas mark 6 (400 °F) (200 °C)

Start by rolling the pastry out thinly, then using a 3¼-inch (8 cm) fluted cutter cut out little circles and place them in tartlet tins. You should get approximately sixteen.

Now, in a bowl, combine the curd cheese, caster sugar, lemon rind, ground almonds and currants, then beat the egg and egg yolk together and add this as well. Mix, very thoroughly, with a fork until everything is evenly blended. Next, spoon the merest trace of jam into the base of each pastry case, then fill each one about two-thirds full with the cheese mixture. When all the mixture has been added, bake them in the centre of the oven for about 25 minutes by which time the mixture will have puffed right up and turned a lovely golden brown. Then take them out of the oven and transfer them on to a wire rack to cool. Don't worry as you see the centres starting to sink down because that's absolutely correct and normal. When they're cool they'll look nice with a faint dusting of icing sugar sprinkled over.

INDEX

INDEX

NOTES

NOTES

NOTES

NOTES

NOTES

NOTES